"Making a pivot isn't a choice, it's necessary for you to grow. *Jump* is the definitive guide to making a career pivot, and I am honored to have received Kim Perell's personal advice during my many pivots."

—ERIC TODA,
Global head of social marketing at Facebook

"*Jump* is a terrific book that will change how you approach your life."

—KARA GOLDIN,
Founder and CEO of Hint, Inc., and *Wall Street Journal*
bestselling author of *Undaunted*

"Kim Perell is the ultimate success story! She has 'jumped' multiple times and has earned the right to speak with authority. She challenges the reader to believe in themselves and walks them through the journey step by step."

—JOHN HEFFNER,
Chairman and CEO of Summer Fridays
and former CEO of Drybar

"With compassion, inspiration, and in-the-trenches wisdom, Kim Perell's book *Jump* is a blueprint for anyone ready to take a personal or professional leap."

—WADE OOSTERMAN,
President of Bell Media and vice chairman of Bell Canada

"I'd recommend *Jump* to anyone looking to make a real change in their life, whether personal or professional. Kim Perell's inspirational and motivational book gives readers actionable steps to identify what change they want to make, overcome their doubts, and gain the confidence and courage needed to take action."

—JONATHAN AUERBACH,
Chief strategy, growth, and data officer at PayPal

JUMP

Dare to Do What Scares You
in Business and Life

KIM PERELL

HARPERCOLLINS
LEADERSHIP

AN IMPRINT OF HARPERCOLLINS

Published by HarperCollins Leadership,
an imprint of HarperCollins Focus LLC.

Any internet addresses, phone numbers, or company or product information printed in this book are offered as a resource and are not intended in any way to be or to imply an endorsement by HarperCollins Leadership, nor does HarperCollins Leadership vouch for the existence, content, or services of these sites, phone numbers, companies, or products beyond the life of this book.

ISBN 978-1-4002-2945-1 (eBook)

ISBN 978-1-4002-2921-5 (HC)

Library of Congress Control Number: 2021942660

Printed in the United States of America

21 22 23 24 25 LSC 10 9 8 7 6 5 4 3 2 1

To my four children,
John, Elle, Bill, and Jack.
I hope you always choose to JUMP
rather than stand still.

CONTENTS

LETTER TO THE READER

Dear Courageous Reader,

Are you hungry for a new career, ready to start a business, or eager to rewrite the script life has currently given you? You already know the next step you have to take is actually not just a step, but a . . . *jump*. A big leap into the unknown.

And that feels a little scary, doesn't it? I know because I've been there myself. Fear of the unknown is normal, and it happens to all of us. I'm also willing to bet that you're feeling something more than fear; your gut is telling you that it's a great idea and that behind the fog of uncertainty, something bigger and better is waiting for you.

I have good news. If your instinct is telling you that it's time to make a change in your life, I wrote this book for you. No matter where you are personally, financially, or emotionally, I promise I've got your back. I know what to do in these heart-racing, palm-sweating, teeth-grinding situations. This book will guide you through the life-changing decisions you want to make. It will provide you with actionable steps to make a change, overcome your doubts, and find the courage to take calculated risks that will pay off big.

I will share lessons and insights from more than twenty years of experience as an entrepreneur, executive, and investor making the hard decisions and finding the courage to jump. I'll reveal the mistakes I've made—many of which could have been avoided—as well as the lessons I've learned and the shortcuts to success that no one tells you.

This book is about learning to take the leap with courage and confidence. No longer do you have to feel stuck. It's time to move forward.

There's no better time to jump than right now. The question is, are you ready to take the leap?

I know you are. And I'm here to help.

Let's jump!

Kim

CHAPTER

1

TAKE THE LEAP

It's scary looking down. Especially when there's a lot at stake.

You know those decisions that make your heart race and your palms sweat? The ones that are so overwhelming you start asking yourself, *how in the world did I even get into this position in the first place?* I do. I've felt that way many times before. I'm a successful entrepreneur now, but that wasn't always the case. I had to take a lot of risks and leap off a lot of cliffs to get here . . . and even now I still get that heart-racing, palm-sweating sensation before I jump into a new adventure.

Every great story starts with a jump—a risk, leaping into the unknown, not knowing exactly how you will land. Whether you're jumping from a place of greatness, from rock bottom, or you're simply stuck, you can absolutely create positive, transformative change in your life. You just have to be willing to trust yourself and take the leap.

THREE REASONS TO JUMP

Before you dive in, it's important to know what type of jump you are taking and why. As a seasoned jumper, I've noticed that there are three main reasons people take big leaps.

Reason #1: You Have No Other Choice

The Survival Jump. You are forced to change. You've been fired, bankrupted, or had a life-changing event, or some other environmental force has you in its clutches. This is less of a choice and more of an emergency exit.

Reason #2: You See an Opportunity

The Opportunity Jump. You want to change because you have a vision. You see a way to improve your life through bold action. You're stable or relatively happy now, but you have big dreams, a business idea, or a vision of how you want your life to be. You feel certain you are meant to do something bigger.

Reason #3: You're Stuck

The Stagnant Jump. You're considering a change because you've stagnated, are bored, or feel unfulfilled. You've reached a certain point in your career where you aren't sure what to do next. You feel comfortable but not challenged. Think of it as a plateau. You stay put because that feels easier than jumping into the unknown.

Here's a little secret: your reason for jumping doesn't matter; the only thing that matters is that you have the courage to take the leap.

SURVIVAL JUMPERS

The Survival Jump I was forced to take early in my career felt like the worst thing that had ever happened to me, but it turned out to be the best. It was the catalyst that changed the course of my life for the better. And between us, I wouldn't be writing this book if I hadn't taken that Survival Jump.

Picture this: I'm twenty-two years old, living in sunny Los Angeles, living in an apartment with my two best friends. I'd just landed my dream job at a new tech startup. It was the peak of the internet bubble, when any company with a ".com" was a hot commodity. I was on top of the world. I was elated and convinced that I'd won the lottery with a new job that would help me thrive and grow during the first stage of my adult life. It was an era of abundance. The money being poured into internet companies was skyrocketing. Big fancy offices, flashy cars, 24/7 parties with champagne and sushi; it was a college grad's dream. The future seemed limitless, and I had a golden ticket.

I was so excited about the opportunity that I convinced my closest friends to come work with me. Unfortunately, the fantasy and promise of this new job and incredible company didn't last long. The company was a precursor to Dropbox (just a decade too early). Data storage costs were high, customer adoption was extremely slow, and our expenses outpaced our revenue. While the advertising division of the company was experiencing impressive levels of growth, the company's core business was bleeding money. I'd worked tirelessly building and running our digital ad sales team—working late nights and weekends, pouring my heart and soul into my work—but our success wasn't nearly enough to keep that sinking ship afloat. With no cash and a failing business model, I was forced to fire all my friends right before I was fired myself. My "dream job" quickly turned into my worst nightmare.

Suddenly I was unemployed, broke, and devastated. I was convinced I'd reached my lowest point. I went home, turned off the lights, crawled into bed, and cried. I don't think I left my room for days. My roommates tried to cheer me up, but I just wanted to be alone. I ate more tubs of Ben & Jerry's than I'd like to admit. I called my mom every day to share my disappointment and fear. Every day, I questioned what I was going to do with my life and wondered if I was a complete failure. I'd hit rock bottom.

Even in the face of all that bleakness and disappointment, I knew if I stood still—if I let my fear and disappointment consume me—my entire future would be in jeopardy. I needed to get my life back on track and take control of my destiny. I was gearing up for the most transformative jump of my career.

Up until this point in my life, every jump I'd taken had been a proactive choice—Opportunity Jump. I was accustomed to taking calculated risks when I saw opportunities or felt ready for a change. (That trait is in my DNA. It's something I'd been doing naturally since I was a kid.) But the jump I was about to take was different. It was completely reactive: a Survival Jump. The rug had been ripped out from underneath me, and I had to make some huge changes—and make them fast.

Knowing myself, I recognized that letting this setback derail my life completely would cause me *more* fear, angst, and misery than gathering my courage and taking a big risk. One late night, eating pizza with my roommates, I made a joke about starting my own business. But my two best friends didn't laugh; they thought it was a great idea. Which made me genuinely ask myself, *wait, what if I did?*

Even though I'd grown up in a family of entrepreneurs, I'd never thought of starting my own business before that moment. As a new college grad, I believed that working for an established company was the most secure path to success. I had been on the entrepreneurial roller-coaster ride with my father growing up, and I didn't like the unpredictability and constant letdowns that came along with it.

I knew better. There were no guarantees, whether you worked for yourself or someone else. This was the hardest lesson. The only thing I knew was I had to try something different. So I started thinking about launching my own digital advertising company. Digital advertising was becoming more mainstream, and even though my startup employer had imploded, the digital advertising division had been solid. Moreover, I was good at it and I loved doing it. I decided to go all in on the digital ad trend. I had built up a solid client list of advertisers, I had experience running a team, and I had serious hustle.

I chose to ignore my excuses. Sure, I might fail, but I had failed already. So, if I was going to fail again, it was going to be on my own terms.

When I started telling more people about my business idea, the reception I received wasn't exactly enthusiastic. And what I mean by that is . . . most thought I was making a massive mistake. I was told I was too young, I had no experience running a company, the timing was wrong, the idea was outlandish, and the chances of success were slim. The adults I told were even more conservative; they said I should scrap my idea, play it safe, and go get a "real" job. (Which confused me because the job I'd just gotten fired from *was* "real"!) Looking back, that makes perfect sense: the market was a graveyard of failed internet companies, the entire economy was in rough shape, and my track record wasn't exactly overflowing with wins (yet!).

Maybe I was crazy. I *definitely* have a streak of craziness. But that's what gives me confidence. In the face of all that uncertainty, I still believed in the opportunity.

Although the dot-com crisis was a wake-up call, I still believed in the potential of a digital business. People assumed that when the bubble burst, the internet was dead too... but very soon afterward, it became more popular than ever. Everyone I knew was spending more and more time online; even my grandma had an AOL account! My gut told me that if I could muster up the courage to start my own business now—while everyone else was fleeing from new endeavors and startups—I had a shot at success. I could let the circumstances of the world define me, or I could take my career and destiny into my own hands and create the future I wanted. I chose the latter. I sat down at my kitchen table, set up my home office, and took the jump that started my journey into entrepreneurship.

It wasn't an easy journey, nor was it a straight line to success. In fact, the line looped up and down with frightening unpredictability, but I wouldn't trade that roller-coaster ride for anything. It was the wild and winding path that shaped me, taught me, and turned me into an entrepreneur—and human being—who embraces opportunity and always chooses to jump rather than stand still.

And it all started because I hit rock bottom.

That lonely, hopeless place is where so many find themselves at some point in their lives. I'm sure many people around you have felt this way—during the recessions of the dot-com bust in the early 2000s, the 2008 financial crisis, and, most recently, the COVID-19 pandemic that caused an unprecedented global shutdown. Rock bottom is a place that plenty of people have been before.

And if there's just one piece of wisdom I want you to take away from this book, it's this: if you've got to jump, rock bottom is a great place to start. After all, there's nowhere to go but up.

The Survival Jump is just one way to jump, but you don't need to be pushed off a cliff to make a life-changing leap.

OPPORTUNITY JUMPERS

Nancy Twine is an incredible example of someone who recognized an opportunity and jumped—*big*. After a seven-year career at Goldman Sachs, she took an Opportunity Jump and left her high-paying Wall Street career to become the CEO of Briogeo Hair Care, now one of the fastest growing hair-care brands at Sephora.[1]

Nancy had been creating her own homemade organic hair-care products for years, using recipes inspired by her grandmother. She found that the hair-care industry was underserved, and she saw that there was opportunity for a newcomer. So she jumped at the opportunity. Nancy presented her products at a beauty trade show and received her first round of purchase orders from retailers like Urban Outfitters. Six months later, Sephora called.

"I know how discerning the merchant team is at Sephora, and having their buy-in to my wild idea really meant a lot to me," said Twine. "I knew that this was my big opportunity, and I had to go for it."[2]

Nancy took the Opportunity Jump to become a clean-beauty entrepreneur and followed her dream of pioneering a transformational brand for all hair types and textures. She is projected to generate $40 million in sales in 2021.

Nancy began with zero experience in the beauty industry, but she has since become a leader in green beauty *and* the youngest Black woman to launch a line at Sephora. Nancy continues to pay it forward, elevating other founders and women of color by mentoring and advising young entrepreneurs through Sephora's Accelerate incubator program.

Like most of the entrepreneurs I know, Nancy had the power of seeing something not as it is, but as the potential of what it could be.

STAGNANT JUMPERS

Chances are that if you are stagnant, you already know. If you dread Mondays, live for the weekend, or have to force yourself out of bed; if you are stuck or bored out of your mind; if you are miserable in your job or see no upward trajectory in your career, you're probably a Stagnant Jumper. Let's address the dangers of stagnation. It's clear that stagnation is the exact opposite of what you've set out to achieve by reading this book. We all know monotony is the death of creativity.

In my experience, there's no growth in the comfort zone, and if you want to overcome stagnation, you need to change.

Let me prove it to you.

A decade after starting my company from my kitchen table and selling it to Singtel, one of the most prestigious telecommunications companies in the world, I decided to take a jump and step down as CEO.

It's never easy to leave a company, especially one that you built from the ground up. I loved my job, the ever-changing environment of the digital world, and the company I worked for. I loved my team of over one thousand talented colleagues around the world, many of whom I considered lifelong friends. And I loved the financial security of being owned by a large, publicly traded company in Singapore.

The easy thing would have been to stay. It was comfortable, but that comfort was starting to become a problem. My gut knew it was time to move on. I tried to ignore the feeling for some time, but eventually, it became impossible. You know the feeling? When your heart knows it's time to go and your brain tries to convince you to stay? It's scary to leave a secure position, but I knew in my gut it was the right decision.

I had an entrepreneurial itch that I just couldn't scratch. I tried to subdue it by investing in startups, sitting on boards, advising founders, and speaking to entrepreneurs. But the drumbeat continued to get louder. I thrive on newness, change, and challenge, and I'm always happier making a somewhat risky decision than allowing myself to become stagnant. I love to embrace the unknown and create something from nothing. And I had a burning desire to do it all over again. It was clear I needed to jump.

So, after a decade, I left my company, took some time to enjoy the special moments of being home each day with family, and then refocused my energy on deciding what I would do next. I loved the digital world, but over the years I'd discovered that my true passion was supporting entrepreneurs, especially helping founders bring their dreams to life.

In September of 2020, I decided to pack up my whole life in San Diego—the home where I built my life and career—and move to Miami to start my new company, 100.co. I believed there was an opportunity to use technology to reinvent how consumer brands are created for the next generation. With four kids aged six and under, I wanted to make sure the products I created were safe, environmentally friendly, and connected to an important cause.

I made this life-changing jump in the middle of a global pandemic. It was a time when most things in the world felt uncertain. It was an election year. The middle of hurricane season in Florida. I didn't have any family in Miami, and I'd spent less than ten days there my entire life.

On the surface, it sounds like a crazy idea. Arguably, insane. But I did what I always do: I trusted my gut. As I write this, my new company is still in its early stages, but every move I've made has felt exciting, rewarding, and just plain right. The first few partnerships I've forged have been with people who are passionate, purpose driven, and socially conscious. I already know I've made the right decision. This jump was exactly what I needed to scratch that itch!

The fact that I did it during a time of real upheaval shows that there is never a perfect time to take a life-changing jump. You will never feel perfectly ready. Big changes are scary, they take resources and planning, and they can be incredibly challenging to put into motion. But they are possible. And they can be achieved if you are committed and courageous.

Only you have the power to change your life.

If you're not excited about your job, start looking for another one. If your skills aren't being used, ask your boss for more responsibility or start looking for another opportunity that puts your talents to better use. If you're physically, emotionally, or mentally exhausted all the time, this is a sign to make a change. It may take time to plan your jump, but the time to start making that plan is now. You must decide to stop stagnating and start planning the next stage of your career, your life, and your future. Like me, you must choose to pull yourself out of the quicksand.

Of course, that quicksand is always waiting to drag down more victims, and individuals aren't the only ones who are susceptible to the dangers of stagnation; great companies fall prey too. Remember Kodak? That legacy American corporation was founded in 1888 and became instrumental in making film photography accessible to regular folks. You probably knew that already . . . but did you know that Kodak invented the digital camera? That's right; twenty-four-year-old electrical engineer Steven Sasson invented the self-contained digital camera at Eastman Kodak in 1975. Unfortunately, his bosses were so focused on their thriving film business that they ignored the possibilities in digitalization. Their competitors, however, didn't. Now Kodak is a ghost of its former self. Once a leader in their industry, they let stagnation get the better of them.[3]

Successful people are constantly observing the world around them and contemplating their next move. They know that change begets change and that it's much easier to switch directions or strategies when you're already on the move. Whether they're artists, politicians, entrepreneurs, or scientists, these successful individuals recognize that big changes in one area of life can spark *more* changes in *other* areas. They see that change makes them more flexible and exposes them to new experiences and new people. It opens doors to more opportunities.

One of my favorite authors and investors, Robert Kiyosaki, once said, "The biggest risk a person can take is to do nothing." I completely agree.

Sometimes we forget we have choices. Remind yourself of your power by making one, purposefully and mindfully. When you make a decision, you take control of your life and your destiny. So change careers if you're in a stagnant job, break up with your significant other if you're in a toxic relationship, start a new business, or move to Miami—whatever it takes to shake things up in your life and remind yourself that you're in control.

Stagnation is death. And change isn't nearly as scary as it might seem on the surface.

LOOK BEFORE YOU LEAP

Before you take a life changing leap, I want you to make sure you're prepared to jump. I promise that the *last* thing I want to do is to make you hesitate. My whole philosophy is that execution is the key to success, and I value progress over perfection. I want you to do, to start, and to act!

But I *don't* want you to fall on your face or hit a wall just as you're building momentum. Changing your life is about overcoming fear and shifting your mindset, but it is also important to look before you leap. Let's take a minute to talk about how to jump into your change with your eyes wide open.

Jumping doesn't have to be an all-or-nothing proposition. You don't have to quit your day job *before* you start planning your startup launch. You don't have to tell your whole family you're moving to London before you've even found a place to live or bought your plane ticket. There's nothing wrong with having a backup plan, or a safety net, or both. Taking the leap doesn't mean making rash decisions that leave you with no security. It means being brave and responsible at the same time. It means assessing the risks, rewards, and repercussions of your actions.

Here are a few questions I ask myself before jumping.

1. *What's the worst that could happen?*
   Back when I'd just launched my first company and was considering buying a house, I found myself hesitating. I got on the phone with my dad, and, as he'd done with me a million times before, he asked me to think about the worst possible outcome if I took this leap. I said, "Well, the company could fail, I could go bankrupt, and I'd have to give the house back to the bank." He asked me, "So is it worth that risk?" It was. So I did it, and I can tell you it was definitely the right decision.
   - Try not to drive yourself into a panic, but do your best to articulate the worst, ugliest, most dire scenario that could result from your jump. Then imagine the best that could happen. Is the positive possibility more powerful than the negative?

2. *Who else will my actions affect?*
   It's *much* easier to jump into huge, life-altering changes if you don't have any dependents. If you're young, unmarried, and without kids, and if none of your other family members or friends depend on you for support or income, you've got a lot of leeway. But your choices might still impact coworkers, colleagues, or investors. So ask yourself these follow-up questions: How will your jump impact the

people in your life? If your choice affects them negatively, what's the worst that can happen *to them*? How about the best?

3. *Who has done this before?*
   Since jumping almost always means trying something that's new to you, consider connecting with someone who already knows the ropes. Can you talk with someone about their experience in this field or someone who has made this change in their own life? Getting their input and advice may help build your confidence, warn you about some pitfalls, or both!

4. *What are my strengths and superpowers?*
   You're about to drastically alter your life. Before you do that, take stock of all the positives. Do you have expertise, education, a network of smart people, a supportive partner? Do you have the ability to talk your way out of tight spots or a talent for predicting successful products? Before you leap, make a list of the things that will bring you comfort and support as you dive into uncertainty.

5. *Can I see my first three steps onto this path?*
   You don't need to see the end of the road, and you don't even need a complete map of the journey! All you need is a rough sense of your first few related actions and enough confidence in yourself to choose the next ones when the time comes.

6. *Am I prepared to navigate unpredictability?*
   Things *will* go wrong after you jump. This is not a possibility; it's a certainty! So ask yourself how you feel about setbacks,

roadblocks, and errors. Are you good at pivoting? What can you do to prepare yourself for unexpected challenges?

In addition to this mental prep, I'm strongly in favor of a backup plan. If you're going to jump, you need to pack a parachute.

A few years ago, my husband, John, decided he was going to master skydiving. One day I found him meticulously rolling his massive sixty-foot parachute across our living room floor into a compact bundle, so he could then fit it into a tiny canvas backpack. To be honest, my anxiety was not eased by him teaching himself how to do this by watching YouTube tutorials.

"What on earth are you doing?" I asked.

"Well," he said, "I'd just rather pack it myself. That way if something goes wrong, I'll know why. And have no one else to blame."

I shook my head and laughed at the time, but I knew exactly what he meant. When you're preparing to jump, you're the only one who really understands what you need. You are making a bet on yourself. No one else can be trusted to pack your suitcase or sketch out your business plan or write your letter of resignation. No one else can formulate your backup plan because you, and only you, know where you can compromise and where you must stand firm. The tools and friends and assets you need in order to feel prepared may be completely different from those that someone else might want in a similar situation. So pack your own parachute, and trust yourself to do it right.

It's important to remember that your backup plan doesn't need to be the classic "six month's salary in the bank." And you don't need a lawyer-approved five-year business plan to launch a company. I talk with too many entrepreneurs who never start because they want to have their entire plan worked out. On the flip side, I've talked with countless others who had an initial plan, took the jump, and made it happen. What you need is a sense of the things that are most likely to go wrong first, and some solid ideas about how you'll handle those missteps. For example, if you're starting a business, ask yourself these questions:

- Where will you land? Might you need a place to crash? Do you have relatives nearby? Friends with comfy couches? A tent and a state-park permit?

- What's your backup? If you need to make ends meet for a while, what skills can you fall back on? Can you tend bar or wait tables? Which temp agencies will you apply to? Can you pick up some freelance work?

- How big is your chute? Do you know how much money you spend each month? What's the minimum amount you need to make it through a month? And I mean eating Top Ramen, canceling cable, and taking the bus everywhere; no-frills living.

A good backup plan is like a mental, logistical, and financial Swiss Army knife. Regardless of how nasty the situation becomes, you have this set of money, ideas, and skills that will help you stay afloat, be safe, or bail if you need to. Your knife might have a file where someone else's has scissors, and that's just fine. The point is to tailor everything to yourself and your unique needs.

If packing your own parachute and formulating your backup plan devolves into procrastination and foot-dragging, force yourself to remember your *best*-case scenario. Acknowledge that, without risk, there is no reward. And when you feel yourself starting to backpedal, remember that this preparatory work is meant to help you feel more prepared to jump.

If you're still hesitating, consider this: the number one regret that people express in their last moments of life is that they left so many important things undone.[4] People wish they'd had more courage, taken more risks, and chased their dreams with more conviction.

Taking the leap may be scary, but regret is scarier. So pack that parachute, take a deep breath, and *jump*.

Chapter 1 Jump Prep

- Identify your reason for making a jump. What are the forces in your life that brought you to this turning point?

- Answer the six questions in the chapter section "Look Before You Leap." Write out your answers, and give them the careful consideration they deserve.
  - (Side note: multiple studies have shown that taking notes with pen and paper helps us process and remember the information more fully than typing it, so consider writing in a journal instead of on your laptop![5])

- Create a solid backup plan. Sure, you might have considered some options; now it's time to take action on them. For instance, instead of just noting that you could crash with your old roommate, text them and ask if they'd be comfortable letting you couch-surf sometime. Yes, write it out, but also do any permission asking or logistical legwork to make it a genuinely actionable plan.

Chapter 1 Jump Hacks

- The jump you're pondering is a big one, right? To work your way up to it, start taking some micro-jumps! Do things that scare and challenge you: sign up for a public speaking class, ask out your crush, introduce yourself to a stranger.

- Find a quote about courage or risk that resonates with you, and put it somewhere you can see it every single day.

It can be a framed watercolor or a sticky note—doesn't matter! Just keep it in view. Here's one of my favorites from Eleanor Roosevelt: "You gain strength, courage, and confidence by every experience in which you really stop to look fear in the face. You are able to say to yourself, 'I have lived through this horror. I can take the next thing that comes along.' You must do the thing you think you cannot do."[6]

CHAPTER

2

MASTER YOUR MINDSET

When I was ten years old, both my brother and my twin sister got into my school's Talented and Gifted program (TAG). The only one who didn't get into the program in my family . . . was me. Twice a week I'd have to swallow my pride and watch my siblings take the "smart kids" bus to the TAG program after school while I stayed back. My twin sister would wave goodbye to me from the back of the bus as I sat on the curb, trying to hide my tears.

I remember a friend thinking it was funny to say, "You're clearly not the smart one." This haunted me. Did it mean I was destined for failure? Totally lacking in talents and gifts? What did these test results really understand about *my* potential? My mom saw me struggling and assured me that I was smart, talented, and deeply worthy. Just because my gifts couldn't be measured by a pen-and-paper test didn't mean they weren't there! She urged me not to compare myself to anyone else, especially my twin sister. She even gave me a mantra to say when self-doubt crept in: "Comparison is the thief of joy" (a nugget of wisdom from Theodore Roosevelt). She taught me that simply shifting my mindset could make the biggest difference in my life. She taught me that my own thoughts and beliefs could shape who I would become.

I still use that mantra, because your mindset is the most important predictor of your success and happiness in life. Change your mindset and change your life.

One of the most important factors influencing a person's success—whether it's personal or professional—is mindset. Your mindset is your thoughts and beliefs about your own abilities. Think of it as the lens that you observe the world through. Although your environment and experiences shape you as a person, your mindset about those experiences impacts how you process them. Your mindset plays a critical role in how you cope with life's challenges and how you feel about yourself and your accomplishments.

In fact, if I had to guess, I'd say it's not logistics, money, or anything concrete that's held you back so far; it's your fears, feelings, and thoughts. Mindset may be a huge reason you haven't taken your jump yet.

You may have had a life-changing jump queued up inside your heart for ages, but every time you reach the cliff's edge your head yanks you back. Your internal dialogue and emotional framework guide your whole life, and if they're guiding you *away* from a big jump, then no amount of advice, logic, or support from trusted friends will get you to take action.

The good news is this chapter will help you recalibrate your mindset. You're going to get more confident internalizing risk and embracing change. I also teach you tools that align your heart and head so you can jump with conviction.

Let's start by ditching the excuses that hold you back!

DELETE YOUR EXCUSES

Excuses are poison. The mile-long list of reasons you can summon up to justify your fears and "protect" yourself from risk will slowly destroy your dreams. But if you learn to obliterate those excuses whenever they arise, you'll soon be able to ditch the fears they represent.

Let's walk through four of the biggest excuses people make that prevent them from jumping.

Excuse #1: I'm Scared I'll Fail

This is the number one reason why people hesitate to make their jumps. But I'll tell you a secret: failure is inevitable. I learned this at a young age. When I was growing up, my dad always asked me, "What's the worst thing that happened to you today?" It's a weird thing to ask, but he did it for a reason. He was building my resilience and making me stronger. I'd tell him my latest humiliating failure, and he'd tell me his.

"Mine's so much worse than yours, Kim. Wait till you hear what happened to me today."

My family would celebrate who had the worst failure. We normalized failure and developed a tolerance for it because that took away its power and mystery. Normalizing it made the potential of failure less terrifying.

Decades later, I called my dad to share one of my latest setbacks. I won a big global deal that was going to give the company enough cash to operate for an entire year, and, at the same time, one of my key, longtime employees, the engineering lead we needed to build the contract we had just closed, resigned. How was I going to deliver on the contract without him? How could I do *anything* without him? The whole deal was resting on having a killer engineering leader, which I was now missing. I was so sure my failure couldn't be beat. *There's no way Dad can top this*, I thought to myself. But he proved me wrong.

He said, "Well, Kimmy, nice try. That sounds rough, but I've got you beat."

There was no way. What could have possibly gone worse for him that day?

He said, "I couldn't make payroll yesterday. So I was actually about to call *you* to ask for a loan."

Needless to say, he won that one. But he didn't let that failure—or any other one he'd face over the course of his career—stop him. I gave him the loan, he paid payroll, and he got his business back on track.

What have I learned from my dad? Failure hurts. Badly. Failure is inevitable. You can't stop it. Failure will knock you down. But when you get knocked down, you have to get back up *and* keep going.

Excuse #2: I Don't Have Enough Time

My dad always believed that eight hours was only half a day of work. Growing up, when I got home from school, he would ask, "What are you doing for the rest of the day?" (Which, in dad-speak, meant: get a job!) I worked at a pizza parlor, putting toppings on pizzas and cleaning plates. I worked at a local candy store while I studied. I folded shirts and stocked inventory at The Gap. I sold suits at Nordstrom. Throughout my young life, I worked my way up the after-school job ladder!

Not having enough time was an excuse that my dad deleted before I could even use it.

If you spend eight hours sleeping and eight hours working, you've still got eight hours of opportunity. What are you doing during your eight hours of freedom? Even if you lop off two hours for things like exercise, cooking, and errands, you've still got six free hours! Being a caretaker or parent requires time; I get it, I have four children myself, so I have to wake early and keep working after they go to bed. Working two jobs to make ends meet *also* requires time, so if you're in that position you'll need to get creative about maximizing your hours and earnings. But if, like many people, you spend your spare eight hours watching TV, playing video games, or scrolling through social media, you can reprioritize that time to focus on your goal.

Start small. Dedicate thirty minutes per day, in the morning or evening, a week to working toward your long-term goals and jump-prep. You'll be amazed how quickly that time adds up . . . and will probably find yourself wanting to carve out even more! Just chip away at those eight hours of opportunity as much as you can, given your responsibilities and constraints.

Excuse #3: I Don't Have Enough Money

This is an excuse that pops up frequently when I speak to aspiring entrepreneurs. My tendency is to push back by asking, "What do you need this money for?" It's one thing if you're planning to launch a restaurant or a product line and need capital for supplies, ingredients, rent, or production costs. But in an era when many businesses can be run entirely online, you can launch something new with a couple hundred dollars in your bank account. Start by marketing through social media, doing skill-swaps with friends to get your infrastructure and website up and running, and handling as much of the initial work yourself as humanly possible.

Of course, I'm strongly in favor of actively saving money! If saving has always been a challenge for you, tackle it just as you did with carving out time: slowly and consistently. Put aside fifty dollars per week or 5 percent per paycheck or whatever small amount you can commit to on an ongoing basis. Create a separate savings account for this money so you won't be tempted to use it on other expenses, and watch that balance grow.

You can do all this on the side while working full-time. Build slowly, be patient, and when your side hustle is bringing in enough revenue, *then* you can make your jump!

Excuse #4: I Don't Have Enough Experience

Take it from someone who launched an online advertising company from her kitchen table after just a few years in the workforce: "I don't have enough experience" is not a good excuse. We live in a time when there are unlimited resources to help you get the skills and expertise you need. The internet has answers, courses, and online groups to help you fill the gaps in your experience. Couple that with asking mentors, friends, and coworkers for their advice. Everyone has to start somewhere, so don't let a lack of experience stop you.

New York Times bestselling author Jenny Lawson shares a story about recording the audio version of her first book, *Let's Pretend This Never Happened*, and what it took for *her* to keep going despite inexperience:

You could hear the trembling in my voice on every word.... I excused myself to get a drink but secretly I was emailing my friend, Neil Gaiman, to ask him how he managed to record so many of his books while still sounding so cool and collected. His response came back almost immediately: pretend you're good at it.[1]

For the first few years of my career, "Pretend you're good at it" was my slogan. Starting a new business means you are constantly walking into new situations. I remember a super-challenging negotiation with a potential business partner early in my career when I felt really inexperienced. I had an important meeting with the CEO of a large company at an annual trade show. The company had rented a large meeting space with numerous soundproof meeting rooms, and sitting in one of these small, weirdly quiet spaces I felt myself starting to sweat. Bright lights pointed down on me from the ceiling as I sat across from the CEO, his attorney, and the head of business development. I wasn't sure if it was a meeting or an interrogation. The company was large and I felt tiny, but I did my best to act as if I would be the best partner they could get. Despite my lack of experience, I told them that working with me would contribute to their business's success. (Which turned out to be true!) The deal got done, and I'm sure those executives had no clue that was my first time in a high-stakes negotiation. I pretended I was good at it, and it worked.

Successful leaders and entrepreneurs are experts at deleting excuses. Just take a look at James Dyson, inventor of the top-of-the-line vacuum cleaner. He spent more than a decade building prototypes—many of them made from cardboard and tape—before he finally mastered his design and built the perfect vacuum.[2]

"It didn't happen overnight, but after years of testing, tweaking, fist-banging, and after more than 5,000 prototypes, it was there," Dyson said. "Or nearly there. I still needed to manufacture it and go sell it."[3]

Potential buyers recognized the machine as pure genius. It was the first innovation that ensured the device would never lose suction—a revolution at the time. Yet the vast majority were too afraid to invest. When a Japanese company finally took the plunge, the first Dyson vacuum hit the shelves. In 1986, the Dyson G-Force sold for $2,000 (which was a small fortune at the time), and the design was so smart it even doubled as a tabletop to save space in tiny Japanese homes.[4] What started as a spendy status symbol in a single country began to win prestigious design awards and gain global attention. By the 1990s, Dyson was a household name, and his vacuums were being sold around the world.[5]

Dyson could have quit at prototype 4,783. He could have set aside his vision for a truly revolutionary vacuum when his wife had to start giving art lessons for some extra cash.[6] He could have let excuses overwhelm him after he struggled to find a manufacturing partner. But he didn't. He deleted his excuses and led with his vision; he knew he was onto something great, and he refused to give up, even in the face of relentless frustration and rejection. Now Dyson is worth billions and runs one of the most successful and respected industrial design companies in the world.[7]

So, how do you follow in his fearless footsteps? What's the key to deleting excuses, even giant, terrifying ones?

You can start by being more aware of negativity, anxiety, and frustration. Just notice when those emotions pop up, or when you feel yourself making excuses.

A simple trick I use every time I find myself making an excuse is to ask myself the "real" reason why I can't accomplish something. I write down my excuse on a piece of paper and then ask myself why. Am I afraid of failure, afraid of embarrassment, or afraid of what other people will think? Usually the real reason I make an excuse stems from fear, anxiety, or self-doubt. Excuses are easy. They allow us to stay in our comfort zones.

When you choose to delete your excuses, you're giving yourself the gift of more room and strength and resources to *act*. It is a choice. Consider it your first mindset-mastery assignment to actively choose to eradicate the excuses that have been forcing you to stay still and play small.

It's challenging because, ultimately, we are wired for noticing negativity. If our partner compliments us forty-nine days in a row and then throws out a stinging critique on day fifty, all forty-nine compliments vanish from our minds and hearts. If our annual performance review is glowing except for three minor issues, we may feel like we've failed. We tend to learn from and cling to our negative experiences and allow them to eclipse our positive ones. This tendency is called "negativity bias," and social scientists have found that it is incredibly tough to combat.

Tough, but not impossible! Dr. Margie Warrell, who studies courage in leadership, asserts that negativity bias and a tendency to make excuses can both be combated through mindfulness and gratitude. Just by noticing what we're noticing—both positive and negative—we can deliberately

refocus our attention on uplifting possibilities and steer ourselves away from harmful excuses. In an excuse-busting exercise that Dr. Warrell shares on her website, she points out, "If
one of your excuses is being 'too busy' decide what you are
going to cut back on, or do differently, to create the time you
need to accomplish it."[8]

That point is absolutely key to pushing past excuses:
you've got to be willing to prioritize, even if it means
making some small sacrifices to move yourself forward.
You've got to accept that your jump will be made possible
by the choices you make beforehand, including choosing to divide your time, resources, and energy in new and
potentially challenging ways. You've got to make internal mindset changes now to pave the way for actionable
changes later.

That means finding ways to delete your excuses . . . and
then, with your newly clear mind, envisioning success,
accomplishment, and positive outcomes galore.

VISUALIZE YOUR SUCCESS

Did you know that visualization and mindset work have been
a part of elite sports for decades? I remember reading an arti-
cle about aerial skier Emily Cook just before the Olympics.
She used visualization scripts to prepare herself for the most
daring jump of her career by playing a recording of her own
voice narrating the spine-tingling jump scenario and using it
like a personal virtual reality set to prepare her for a flawless
performance.

New York Times journalist Christopher Clarey interviewed Cook for his piece "Olympians Use Imagery as Mental Training":

"I would say into the recorder: 'I'm standing on the top of the hill. I can feel the wind on the back of my neck. I can hear the crowd,'" Cook said. "Kind of going through all those different senses and then actually going through what I wanted to do for the perfect jump. I turn down the in-run. I stand up. I engage my core. I look at the top of the jump."[9]

But does it really *work*? It sure does. A study conducted by exercise physiologist Guang Yue at the Cleveland Clinic Foundation asked volunteers to imagine flexing their biceps as hard as possible. After a few weeks, his subjects showed a 13.5 percent increase in strength! And, believe it or not, none of the participants physically flexed—they *just* visualized their biceps growing.[10] Visualization is the real deal.

I've often used a similar technique before pitching a prominent investor or trying to close an important deal. I start by visualizing the room. I can see what I am wearing, where I am standing, and the faces of people I know will be there. I think about my tone and who I'd most like to impress, what I want the client or investor to feel as I give my presentation, the applause and handshakes afterward, and the adrenaline rush of success. This simple technique has worked beautifully for me, time after time. I visualize the outcome I want to achieve long before I have achieved it, and that mindset prep paves the way for my success.

Even before I was running my own businesses, I recognized the power of visualization because I grew up using this technique! My mom is a consultant who works with entrepreneurs, and I watched her use this tactic with her clients and bring it into our family's life. As a teen, I remember creating vision boards with my mom every New Year's Day to help us manifest what we wanted to achieve in the year ahead. We'd spend the whole afternoon chatting at the kitchen table, cutting out pictures in magazines, and pasting them into our collages on a poster board. She never gave me a ton of rigid instruction; she just told me to cut out the words and images that sparked excitement and inspiration and that I wanted to have in my own life.

I created my most ambitious vision board the year before I sold my first company in 2008. I used doors to symbolize new beginnings, the word *closed* to evoke the completion of the deal itself, images of people celebrating, and a photo of the beach where I planned to vacation once the deal was done. And I'm not going to lie; I cut out a few pictures of piles of cash. I hung the board across from my desk as a visual reminder to motivate me daily. I knew visualization activated my subconscious mind, and by incorporating visual images and words related to my goal into my direct line of sight, I took more action that was critical to reach them.

I've also used a simpler technique that involves a little less glue than my vision boards: writing down my goal on a sticky note. In 2013, I was ready to sell my business again, so I wrote down the date I wanted to sell it by and the name of the company I wanted to sell it to. I taped it to my bathroom mirror. I looked at it every single day. The sticky note stared at me when I did my makeup and when I brushed my teeth. It became a constant visual reminder of what I wanted to achieve. It got wet and wrinkled, so eventually I had to duct-tape it to the mirror. But that writing on that sticky note ended up being the simplest and most essential thing I did to keep my vision top-of-mind. And nine months later, I sold my business for $235 million.

Today, I still believe in the magic of visualizing who I want to be, a practice that requires a powerful and intentional mindset. The definition of a visionary is someone who sees the way things *could* be, not the way they are. And to do that, you need the right mindset—not one anchored in doubt and fear.

This is all good news: it means that visualization works across all types of situations and can help you accomplish anything from building muscle to building profits. You can literally create your own reality. Changing your thoughts will undoubtedly help you change your life. Envisioning a successful jump will help bring that success into being.

CODING CONFIDENCE

Of course, even with your excuses obliterated and your success envisioned, you may still lack the confidence you need to commit to your jump. You may know intellectually that you're capable of making this momentous change in your life, and you may have taken active steps to clear mental obstacles from your way . . . and you may *still* hit a wall of fear and doubt when you approach the change itself.

Fortunately, confidence is an active choice.

That's right: Contrary to what we've been taught, confidence is *not* a personality trait. No one is born confident. And on the flip side, no one is born totally incapable of building confidence. Self-confidence is generated by the thoughts we think (mindsets!) and the actions we take. Interestingly, it's less about our actual ability to succeed at a task than it is about *our belief in our ability* to succeed.

Skeptical? Science backs me up on this one! A study by researchers from the University of Colorado and University of Western Australia showed that confidence itself doesn't lead to high performance. The opposite is actually true: confidence is the by-product of previous performance.[11] Meaning if you create patterns in your life that allow you to try challenging experiences, do well, and build up memories of your successes, those memories will fill up your confidence tank. Since confidence is directly tied to past performance, it can be practiced and cultivated like any other habit or skill!

So, in advance of your big jump, set up a series of smaller jumps. Prove to yourself that you can do hard things, even if they're minor: set and conquer a fitness goal over the course of a month; do one thing each day that scares you; fix or build something using YouTube tutorials. You may not believe that any of those things will help you launch a new business, leave a toxic relationship, or make a big career move, but I promise they will. They'll affect your mindset and eventually become a running list of accomplishments you can pull up whenever you're feeling unsure. They'll help you focus on what you can do, instead of what you can't.

I experienced the importance of small wins myself toward the beginning of my journey as an entrepreneur. When I first started my company, I would get an automated email every time we made a sale. Whenever an email came sailing into my inbox letting me know that we'd sold one more product, I felt productive, validated, and confident. The sales showed me that, slowly but surely, I was growing and making progress. As the business started to grow, the sales emails became too frequent to track. Eventually we had official celebrations on reaching one thousand sales and ten thousand sales and beyond . . . but before that point, I celebrated each one!

And now, looking back on my journey as an entrepreneur, I still take time to celebrate the small-yet-significant wins on the way to achieving my larger vision. In fact, I seek to actively stockpile my small wins. From my first website to my first paycheck, my first hire, my first sale, my first investor—I savor all of it, because each step is a small success on my journey to my ultimate goal.

If the idea of small wins doesn't resonate for you, there are other ways to build confidence just as quickly. I'm constantly on the hunt for new ways to challenge myself and improve my confidence, and one of my favorites is a bit like exposure training. As a rule of thumb, if something scares me or I hesitate because I haven't done something before . . . I make myself do it! I've reached out to role models I've always been too intimidated to talk to in person. I've volunteered to lead assignments for which I had no experience. I took golf lessons so I could negotiate a hole-in-one business deal. And every time I conquered one of these goals or skills, it boosted my confidence. This technique requires a relatively bold personality—or, at least, a willingness to experiment with boldness temporarily—but I can say from personal experience that it *works*.

Since we're all wired a little differently, there's no one-size-fits-all way to build confidence. It's a tricky trait that simply doesn't stick for some of us, especially if we've faced long strings of setbacks. But since confidence comes from trying and conquering tasks—the experience of success—you can reverse engineer your own confidence-building technique. Try thinking back to your biggest accomplishments or toughest challenges. Why did you decide to do those things? How did you motivate yourself? How did you feel afterward? Is there a way to re-create similar circumstances for yourself now so you can capture that same energy?

I know this sounds like a lot of work, but trust me when I say it's worth the effort. A confident mindset will help you navigate challenges and tackle tough situations with ease. It may not be easy to make that shift toward confidence, but finding a way to do it will make this jump—and every jump you take for the rest of your life—less stressful and more successful.

YOU WILL NEVER BE READY

I don't believe that anyone is ever truly "ready." For anything.

Seriously.

Nobody is ever fully ready.

Do you think that LeBron James waited until he felt fully ready to declare for the draft and play for the Cleveland Cavaliers? Nope. Do you think singer-songwriter Billie Eilish was ready for international superstardom when she started recording songs in her brother's bedroom and uploading them to SoundCloud? Definitely not. Or that Vincent van Gogh waited until he had an art degree and the approval of critics to begin painting? Hard no. All of these people had talent, and all of them spent their time and energy preparing to tackle their ultimate goals. But none of them were totally ready. I guarantee it.

I can relate. I wasn't ready when I launched my first business. I wasn't ready when I bought my first house. I wasn't ready when I had my first set of twins (or my second set!), and I wasn't ready when I moved across the country from California to Florida. But that didn't stop me from taking action. No one is ever 100 percent ready.

And this may sound ironic since you're currently reading my *second* book, but I felt totally unprepared to write my first book, *The Execution Factor*. I had always wanted to write a book, but it seemed so overwhelming. I love helping others succeed and believed many could benefit from the lessons I'd learned and the challenges I'd faced starting my own company. I felt like writing it all down would help give aspiring entrepreneurs a playbook for success and would be the best way to help the maximum number of people.

But what if I poured my heart and soul into a book and no one liked it, or, worse, what if no one read it? Even though I felt that I was far from ready to write a book, I made myself push past my fears. My passion in life is helping others succeed, and if by writing a book I could increase the number of people I helped, it would be worth the discomfort.

The process was extremely challenging but ultimately successful. I was humbled and honored that *The Execution Factor* became a national bestseller and was able to impact so many. If I'd waited until I felt "ready" to write it, I guarantee it never would've been written.

I've seen time and again that great people, successful people, brave people *all* dive into action before they're ready. They all take risks and force themselves to jump without knowing for certain where they'll land. Readiness is a myth. It can even become an excuse, if you let it.

Which is not to say that you should stop looking before you leap! Again, readiness is different from preparation, and there's great value in preparation and formulating a backup plan. You must trust yourself, know your strengths, be willing to improvise, and make compromises on the road to success. You need to have a strong-but-imperfect vision for yourself, believe that you can bring that vision to fruition, and get started on it.

That's how I run my own life.

And with a few key mindset shifts, you can too.

Chapter 2 Jump Prep

- Which of the four excuses is preventing you from your jump? What are you going to do to delete that excuse?

- Try Dr. Warrell's excuse-busting exercise from earlier in this chapter. What change would you like to accomplish? What excuses are getting in your way? What has been the impact of these excuses? What about the payoff? What actions will you take as a result of this exercise? Do you have an upcoming presentation, project, confrontation, or other challenge that's worrying you?

- How do you plan to build your confidence in advance of your jump? If none of the suggestions from this chapter resonated, remember that you can create your own technique. Commit to a confidence plan and take action.

Chapter 2 Jump Hacks

- Visualize: The next time you are gearing up for a stressful or anxiety-producing event, think like an Olympian: visualize yourself succeeding. In the days leading up to the meeting or activity, sit down, close your eyes, and picture yourself being prepared, impressive, bold, and triumphant. Do it all again right before the event itself. You will find it works!

- Make a list of your past accomplishments that you can pull up when you're feeling unsure. Keep it nearby as a highlight reel to reinforce your past success and give you a confidence boost.

- Write down your goal or vision, and place it where you can see it and review it every day. According to David Kohl, a professor at Virginia Tech, people who write down their goals earn nine times as much over their lifetime as people who don't have goals.[12] Don't just think it; ink it!

- Take action: Make a calendar of confidence-building activities for yourself. At least once per week for the next three months, assign yourself a task or project that you can tackle and store into your confidence bank.

  Call your credit card company and ask for a lower interest rate; play a song you wrote at an open mic night; ask your boss for more regular feedback. If it will help cement these wins in your mind, journal about them.

CHAPTER

3

TURN YOUR FEARS
INTO FUEL

In the months leading up to writing this book, I spoke to dozens of people about why they were hesitant to start something new, and their answer was often the same: they were afraid.

I can definitely relate.

When I started my first company, I had dozens of what-ifs swirling around in my head. What if my company fails? What if people laugh at me? What if I can't get customers? What if no one believes in me? What if I don't believe in myself? Sometimes, I wondered if that fear I felt was a sign I just wasn't cut out for starting my own company. But here's the thing: fear is a natural human emotion. Everyone feels fear, especially people who are making transformative changes in their business or personal lives.

Over the years I've learned that the key isn't to magically make your fears go away or pretend they don't exist. In order to succeed at your jump, you have to acknowledge, address, and conquer your fears so they don't control your life.

Here are the five fears every jumper faces (and how to start conquering them):

1. Fear of Failure

Fear of failure is one of the most common phobias, especially among new and aspiring entrepreneurs. In fact, 33 percent of Americans admit that the fear of failure holds them back from starting a business.[1] But despite how terribly final it may feel, failure isn't the opposite of success. Failure is a crucial part of success.

Countless successful people and businesses faced a ton of failures on their road to success. Stephen King received thirty rejection letters for his first novel, *Carrie*, which went on to be a massive bestseller. Abraham Lincoln lost the Senate race of 1858. Michael Jordan didn't make his high school's varsity basketball team the first time he tried out. Failing doesn't make you a failure. Giving up does.

Ask yourself: If I jump, what is the worst-case scenario that could happen if I fail? Could I live with this? Would life go on? Start viewing failure as a chance to learn and grow.

2. Fear of Uncertainty

Resisting change is a natural impulse. We tend to default to what's easiest and most comfortable. We stay at our job because we're scared to start over. We stay in bad relationships because we think it's better than being alone. We fear moving to new neighborhoods and cities because we don't know if we will fit in. We fear speaking up because we're afraid of how other people will respond.

In order for things to get better, they're going to have to change.

Fear of the unknown is so common. But the unknown is only unknown until you know it, and the only way to know it is to move forward and *discover it*. Take risks and move forward with confidence, trusting that you'll figure things out along the way. Acknowledge that, more often than not, life's going to throw you curveballs. The only thing certain in life is uncertainty. But as long as you stay resilient and keep moving forward the best you can, you'll grow, adapt, and become even stronger than you were before.

Think back on the times when things didn't go according to plan. In those situations, how did you adapt and press forward? What skills did you use to succeed, despite the circumstances?

3. Fear of Rejection

On some level, every person on earth is at least a *little* afraid of rejection. When you're about to make your pitch to investors, you might worry they'll laugh you out of the room. When you ask an expert for advice, you might be nervous they'll judge you for being a novice. When you're trying to sell your product or service to your customers, you might be afraid no one will buy it.

In any of those instances, the worst thing that can happen is that they reject you and say no—socially awkward, but not exactly life-threatening. Yet for some reason, contemplating that rejection can feel super scary in the moment.

In business and love and friendship and life, you're going to face your fair share of rejection. But I'm here to tell you that's actually a *good* thing.

You don't need everyone to say "yes" to you. You only need the right people to say "yes" to you.

As you search for an ideal investor who believes in you, that amazing life partner who just gets you, that excellent mentor who has total faith in you, you're going to encounter a lot of people to coach you. But in order to find out whether they are or not, you're just going to have to ask. Don't take it personally when you get a no. You don't want to work with someone who doesn't believe in you or your vision. Be grateful that they didn't waste your time any further with a lukewarm "maybe" or a noncommittal "sure."

To help overcome your fear, try to uncover what it is about rejection that really scares you. Maybe you're afraid of romantic rejection because you hate feeling lonely. Recognizing this can help you prioritize developing strong friendships and reinforcing your family relationships, both of which will help keep loneliness at bay. If you worry about being rejected for a promotion you really want, make a plan B: list out the things that appeal to you about this new position (more responsibility, the chance to be creative, supervising others), and consider ways to fold those things into your current job.

4. Fear of Not Being Good Enough

Sometimes, the hardest person to please isn't an investor or a customer or a partner or a parent.

It's yourself.

So many people struggle with believing they really are good enough to start a business, be successful, and even find happiness. Even when they do experience success, they may feel as though they don't deserve it.

I still experience feelings of self-doubt from time to time. It's hard to stay positive and confident in the face of uncertainty—and any setbacks can feel devastating when you already question your abilities.

Here's my advice to those who struggle with that same fear:

Invest in relationships. Find mentors, peers, and friends who see your potential and genuinely believe you deserve to be where you are. Their belief in you will help give you the confidence to pursue your dreams.

Master your emotions. Fear and self-doubt feel like facts, but really they're merely emotions that are only as powerful as we allow them to be. Acknowledge those feelings for what they are, and try not to let them distort your reality. Learning how to recognize fear for what it is can help you master it.

Stop comparing yourself. Embrace what makes you different, and focus on becoming the best version of yourself. Everyone has their own special talents—the key is to find yours and execute on what you're good at.

The fear of not being good enough is a mindset. No amount of external success will fix it—it's got to come from within. Self-reflection, supportive relationships, and positive self-talk will help you overcome this fear.

5. Fear of Success

As you move forward toward your jump, you'll be facing all kinds of new challenges you've never encountered before. All of the other fears we talked about tend to get magnified as the stakes get higher. You may worry about what will be different in your life if you actually succeed.

Trust that you'll be able to rise to the occasion. Build a team of strong people you can lean on and learn from. Focus on the great things success can offer, such as financial and creative freedom. And allow yourself to celebrate the successes you experience along the way! Enjoy how awesome it is to see your hard work and passion rewarded.

I've felt all five of these fears throughout my life. But I don't let them dictate my life or stop me from moving forward. I'm far more scared of standing still.

All around me, I see people find their own ways to tackle these fears (and more) head-on. Right now, more and more people are facing their fears and making huge positive changes in their lives, just like you. Every day, there are people out there trying new hobbies, reconnecting with childhood dreams, launching businesses, and abandoning toxic relationships. They're seeing that a big change in one area of life can spark more changes in other areas, both professionally and personally.

What I love most about this widespread embrace of change is that people are approaching change with a Beginner's Mind and an openness to more possibilities. This concept originates in Zen Buddhism but can radiate into any area of life where we are facing newness and the opportunity to learn. With a Beginner's Mind, we can dive into new challenges with curiosity, knowing that our lack of experience is actually an asset. It's where the term "fresh perspective" comes from, because that newness can also give us a sense of wonder that seasoned experts sometimes lack.

The world is going through massive changes, so embracing personal transformation is a smart move. It helps you keep pace and stay agile as opportunities arise and conditions shift. Change exposes you to new experiences and new people, and opens doors to new exciting opportunities. The more you do it, the better you get at it, and the more exciting it becomes.

But to reach the point where you find change exciting instead of overwhelming, you need to practice. Learn to embrace uncertainty and use your fear as fuel. To leverage your fears for positive outcomes, you need to push yourself well beyond your comfort zone.

GET COMFORTABLE BEING UNCOMFORTABLE

Humans love comfort. We adore convenience and ease and anything that allows us to put forth minimal effort. We may take the same route to work every morning, have the same coffee order, go to our favorite restaurants and order the same thing on the menu. Sweatpants: forget buttons, just pull 'em on! Microwavable meals: no more ingredients, pots, or dishes!

Of course, being comfortable does not necessarily put us in the position to spawn great ideas or world-changing inventions. Being comfortable is about sitting still, passive acceptance, not rocking the boat. It's the opposite of jumping.

Being uncomfortable is the specialty of pioneers, innovators, and massively successful people. Let's look at SPANX founder Sara Blakely.

Blakely failed the law school admission test twice, worked at Disney World in a chipmunk costume, and then sold fax machines door-to-door for a grueling seven years. She tells horror stories of doors slamming in her face, getting her business card ripped up, and being escorted by the police out of office buildings . . . so she had to overcome her fair share of discomfort as a saleswoman! But over time she became somewhat immune to these negative reactions. Sara realized she was extremely talented at sales; the only problem was she didn't want to sell fax machines anymore. To anyone. Ever again. She daydreamed about selling a product she actually cared about . . . and then that product presented itself to her.

"In the hopes of looking better in my fitted white pants, I cut the feet out of a pair of pantyhose and substituted them for my underwear. . . . The moment I saw how good my butt looked, I was like, 'Thank you, God, this is my opportunity!'"[2]

But with this epiphany came a new kind of discomfort: Blakely had never explored manufacturing a product, she'd never sold anything to department store buyers, and she had $5,000 to her name and zero investors.[3] She'd never gone to business school. She had no idea how to sew, so she could barely make a prototype of the product she was envisioning.[4] She might've been great at selling, but this was brand-new territory. Nevertheless, she dove right in and started researching patents and hatching her plans. She made her first sale to the Neiman Marcus down the street from her apartment, and the rest is history.

Blakely found the supporters and resources she needed to build her company, SPANX, into a billion-dollar business. In 2012, *Forbes* named her as the youngest self-made female billionaire,[5] and she's expanded her offerings to include leggings, swimwear, and maternity wear, all of which is sold in more than fifty countries.[6] She could've kept her discomfort level at "selling fax machines to people who don't want them," but she stepped it up to "selling shapewear to department stores." And by doing that, she hit her stride.

Like Blakely, I believe that getting comfortable being uncomfortable is the best way to build confidence and learn to trust yourself. After all, if you can improvise on the spot without fear of embarrassing yourself, you're basically invincible! When you hit that sweet spot, you know that when embarrassment and rejection come your way, you will survive and you will recover. Being on good terms with your own discomfort gives you more freedom to try new things without agonizing over the possible outcomes.

In my own life, I have learned that being uncomfortable is a sign that I am growing and progressing. If I want to make change in my life, comfort is *not* a good place for me to be. So I've come to embrace change and the uncomfortable emotions that come with it.

Building my first company gave me plenty of opportunities to accept my own discomfort, and to help my employees do the same! In fact, when advertising on Facebook was uncharted territory, I decided to jump headfirst into this new and largely unproven advertising opportunity. I needed someone to lead the charge. There was a relatively new employee whose performance had impressed me already. He was the kind of person that came up with fresh and innovative ideas and then fearlessly implemented them. He had the ambition, professionalism, and passion that I knew would make him successful. So, even though he had limited experience, I decided to offer him this opportunity for growth. Here's how he tells the story:

I was only two years into my role at Kim's company and really just starting to feel comfortable. But little did I know, that feeling of "comfort" would be surprisingly short-lived as Kim approached me at a company event to lead a new opportunity.

"Stefan, I need you to go to San Francisco," she told me. "You are going to represent the company and become our Facebook marketing expert."

What?! My heart raced. First of all, at that time I didn't know Kim very well. Kim is and always was approachable, but she still was the CEO of our company, and when the CEO asks you to do something directly, it can be nerve-racking. I had never been on a work trip, and this felt like a big deal. But in reality, that's not the real reason my fear started to creep in. I was feeling anxious about the unknown. And, unfortunately in situations like this, it's far easier to begin thinking about how you are going to fail than it is to visualize the greatness that can come from a new opportunity.

Before I could respond, Kim asked me: "Stefan, are you going to make a jump in your career, or are you going to keep being comfortable?"

I chose to jump.

A week later, I was in San Francisco becoming an "expert" in Facebook advertising (something I knew nothing about). I learned more in those two days than I had in the previous year. I left San Francisco energized and enthralled by something new. It was honestly amazing.

I had no idea at the time, but my trip to San Francisco and this new opportunity would shape my life forever. I shifted roles to work on this new project exclusively, and it grew faster than anyone expected.

Then I was asked to build a team that would eventually include dozens of members across the globe. When I look back at this experience, I can't help but think, *What if I hadn't jumped?* I could have claimed to be "busy" that week and found a way out of it. I would have missed out on exponential personal and professional growth, countless new friendships across the world, and experiences I will never forget. What I've come to realize is that being uncomfortable is actually *good*. It pushes us to reflect, to grow, to believe in ourselves, and to ultimately capture the feeling of fulfillment we are all so desperately seeking. Because the reality is that being comfortable is great . . . but if you stay comfortable for too long, life becomes boring. What I learned is so simple: get comfortable being uncomfortable. The risk is far less than the potential rewards. You never know how something like a little push can move you toward the most important jump of your life.

Becoming social media experts was a game changer for us. Our success with Facebook became the playbook for every other new advertising channel that was created: Instagram, LinkedIn, Twitter, Snapchat, Pinterest, you name it. And Stefan led the charge! What started with a $5,000 Facebook advertising campaign eventually turned into an annual revenue stream of over $200 million.

My own experiences getting comfortable being uncomfortable have taught me that when you choose bravery over fear, you're winning. When you choose discomfort over the easy path, you're growing. Am I saying that you need to be uncomfortable all the time, or that doing things you excel at has no value? No. All I'm saying is that huge growth, great ideas, and world-changing actions never happen when we're nestled in our comfort zones. We can all learn to value discomfort as a catalyst for change.

Here are some ways to leverage discomfort.

IMMERSE YOURSELF IN DISCOMFORT

You can't banish all discomfort from your life. As appealing as that may sound, it's impossible. And it's also counterproductive! Discomfort is a driver of curiosity, innovation, and *action*. We may not enjoy the sensation, but it can be a positive force in our lives.

Social scientists have investigated the value of discomfort again and again and made fascinating discoveries. Yale researchers found that feelings of uncertainty signal the brain to kick-start learning, and that *stability* is like a shut-off switch canceling out creativity and problem-solving activity.[8] After reading about this, I fell down a research rabbit hole and found this fabulous story: Google engineer Max Hawkins took the study's findings to heart and built an app that would force him into unfamiliar situations.

Max started small, with an app that integrated Uber. . . . He would press a button in the app and a car would arrive. But then, a twist: He couldn't select a drop-off location; the app would choose a spot within a range without disclosing it.[9]

He randomized his life for nearly two years and has written and spoken extensively about how embracing discomfort made him understand himself better, explore the world more boldly, and take control of his choices.[10] Amazing, right? He encourages us to question the things that make us comfortable, since they can lull us into total paralysis.

And there's more! Psychiatrist and neuroscientist Nancy C. Andreasen studies creativity and insists that her most brilliant subjects have all been adventuresome and exploratory by nature, unafraid to confront doubt and rejection; she believes that no genius, alive or dead, has shied away from discomfort.[11] And numerous other studies have shown that the world's most successful salespeople actually *thrive on discomfort*.[12]

I could keep going, but you get the point.

When we're comfortable, we stand still. There's no reason to move or adjust our position. When we're uncomfortable, we know that the only way to improve our situation is to change. If we want things to get better, it's up to us to *make* them better.

Of course, it's a fine line. A little discomfort motivates us, but too much discomfort can paralyze us.

So, how do you find that balance for yourself? Do some self-reflection. It's important to know what makes you uncomfortable and why so you can navigate and manage those feelings. Think about the jump you want to take. Maybe you're moving across the country, quitting your day job to write a novel, or confessing your love to a longtime crush. Whatever you've got planned, hold the situation in your mind. Imagine yourself taking the actions that lead up to the jump itself, and notice when you start to clench your muscles or feel your stomach doing flips. What was the trigger? And what was the feeling? Fear? Anxiety? Embarrassment? Were you concerned that someone you respect would judge you harshly or that you'd get laughed at? Terrified that your idea would flop and you'd end up broke? Is this discomfort about facing one huge unknown factor, or a thousand tiny unknown factors all at once? Unpleasant as it is, try to dig into those details and find the true source of your discomfort.

Don't worry about finding solutions or ways to address the fear. Just give it a name.

Once you have it pinpointed, you automatically have more power over it. You know when that discomfort might pop up and why, and you can bat it down like a game of whack-a-mole. You know that although your feelings are real and valid, they don't need to stop you from moving forward. You know that, no matter its source, your discomfort can be harnessed as a motivator. You can take that energy and, instead of letting it paralyze you, let it catalyze you.

When I started my first business, my team spent more than a year trying to secure a large client that would change the game for us. That target company was larger and more complex than any of the clients we'd landed before. We wanted to aim high and prove to ourselves that we could play in the big leagues. So we spent that entire year making calls, scheduling meetings, and flying to the company's office, only to repeatedly hear the word *no*.

After being refused a dozen times, my team and I went to meet the company's executive team at a conference. We spent the entire presentation sweating as the potential client picked apart our whole business model. But guess what? We closed the deal.

If we hadn't been persistent, despite our numerous failures, we never would have succeeded. And if we hadn't pushed ourselves *way* out of our comfort zones, we never would have landed that game-changing deal.

Now I know that embracing discomfort is much easier when it's done in the name of an Opportunity Jump. Starting a new business, volunteering to lead a big project, or deciding to adopt a child are all challenging changes, but they're also exciting and are things we all do by choice. If your jump is a Stagnant Jump (one that you'll be taking because you're feeling stuck), leaving your comfort zone can feel far riskier. Even if you're taking a Survival Jump (one that you'll be taking because you're being forced to change), you may find yourself thinking, *Better to stick to the devil you know than the devil you don't.* Breaking out of your comfort zone becomes truly terrifying if you've got a lot at risk or if you have no idea what might meet you on the other side of your jump.

I get it, I swear. But I also want to encourage you to jump anyway. Here's why:

I talk with dozens of people who feel stuck in their career every week, and *far* too many of them are trying to escape their misery. They're nurturing dreams of founding a new business or venture because their current circumstances are slowly killing them. If this is you, too, I want you to hear me loud and clear: Any situation that's crushing your soul doesn't deserve you. Whether it's a dysfunctional workplace or toxic relationship, you can and should plan for change. It will be uncomfortable to leave—far, far outside your comfort zone—but you're suffering right now. What is safe or good about suffering? That may be a devil you know, but could that faceless, unknown devil really be worse than staying put?

Recently, I reconnected with an energetic, passionate guy who used to work for me. He had a new job with a fancy title, and when we met for coffee I fully expected to hear about how much he adored his rewarding, thrilling new role. Instead, he told me his job was unspeakably awful and that the fancy title just meant more meetings, more reports, and less of the work he actually loved doing. It broke my heart. And you'd best believe I told him what I'm telling you now: It may take time and energy to plan your exit, but it's worth the effort. It may be uncomfortable to think about the unknown, but if you don't embrace change, nothing will ever get better.

Turning your fears into fuel isn't just about conquering your nerves to try a fun new endeavor; it's also about gearing up for your jump by taking stock of your situation and acknowledging that staying in it will grind you down. It's about accepting that your "comfort zone" isn't actually comfortable, it's just familiar.

And while the unknown may be scary, it might just be marvelous too.

So start researching, start planning, and get ready to jump so you can find out for yourself.

PRACTICE GETTING REJECTED

Let's be honest: rejection hurts. Fear of rejection prevents many talented people with phenomenal ideas from chasing their dreams. It's amazing how much more we value the opinions of others than we value our opinions of ourselves. Just the possibility that peers or investors might judge us is enough to keep us from trying. Fear kills more dreams than failure ever will.

What many of us don't realize is that rejection is also part of living a full, rich, rewarding life. It goes hand in hand with taking risks and being bold, and just like discomfort it can be a great motivator.

Comedian Chris Rock has often shared the story of a rejection experience that changed his life. In the early 1990s, Rock was playing a theater in Chicago, with Martin Lawrence opening for him. He was sitting in his dressing room backstage when he heard what sounded like a fight in the audience, or maybe even a riot. So he looked out from the wings. It was just people losing their minds over Lawrence's set. They were stomping their feet and banging on tables they were laughing so hard.[13] Rock was booked for an hour-long set and says he made it through about twenty minutes of polite laughter mixed with dead silence before slinking off the stage.[14]

He was shaken. He was a *Saturday Night Live* alum with multiple movies under his belt who'd just been shown up by a newcomer.

This was rejection on a grand (and painful) scale.

But Rock put his rejection to good use. He knew that he was amazing at writing jokes, but he resolved to get better at *telling* them. He went all in on this transformation, building a dedicated rehearsal space with mirrors on the walls so he could practice his physical performance and hone his delivery. When he reemerged, he'd forged a bolder, more theatrical delivery style—including his now-famous technique of "stalking" the stage, walking up and down its length to broadcast energy—and his jokes were more attuned to his unique point of view.

The rejection became a blip on the radar of his career. And by using it productively—by turning his fears into fuel—Chris Rock grew into one of the most iconic and beloved comedians in the world.

Just like clothes, rejection comes in all shapes and sizes. You can learn just as much from your biggest rejection as you can from your smallest. And there's no faster way to learn from rejection than by selling something that no one wants to buy. I know this personally because I developed a healthy tolerance for rejection by starting my career in sales. I was selling digital ad space when people were still interested in buying ads in the Yellow Pages, and no one was interested in buying from me! It certainly wasn't enjoyable to get rejected by nearly every customer I contacted, but it taught me three important lessons: that persistence pays off, that the right customer is willing to listen, and that I really, really enjoy the sales process.

As my experience proved, harnessing rejection doesn't have to mean experiencing one giant smack in the face and revising your life in response. It can be a slow burn, a project or ongoing experience where you build up your tolerance to smaller rejections so they aren't as scary when they pop up. Entrepreneur Jia Jiang tried this out and spoke about his experience in a TED Talk, saying, "'Rejection Therapy' was this game invented by this Canadian entrepreneur. His name is Jason Comely. And basically the idea is for thirty days you go out and look for rejection, and every day get rejected at something, and then by the end, you desensitize yourself from the pain." Jiang went above and beyond by seeking out rejection for one hundred days and creating a video blog of his experiences! He set impossible tasks for himself—like borrowing one hundred dollars from a total stranger or asking a random university professor if he could teach class for a day—and the results were reliably hilarious.[15]

But the experiment also had the intended effect on Jiang: he inoculated himself against rejection.

> Rejection was my curse, was my boogeyman. It has bothered me my whole life because I was running away from it. Then I started embracing it. I turned that into the biggest gift in my life. I started teaching people how to turn rejections into opportunities.[16]

Do *you* need to have a mile-long list of nutty ways to get rejected? Nope! But if you're gonna make this jump happen, you need to embrace the idea of rejection and the feeling of being rejected. Practicing being told no or listening to negative feedback in low-risk situations is a fantastic way to remind yourself that rejection is far scarier in your mind than it is in reality. It won't kill you, it won't physically hurt you, and it doesn't even have to *prevent* you from continuing down your chosen path.

So, before you ask for that big promotion, ask for a customer discount at your favorite restaurant. Before you show potential investors your prototype, show your friends and family. Ask a stranger to pay for your coffee. Intentionally put yourself in situations where you may get rejected.

It won't kill you. And it just might make you stronger.

LOVE IT MORE THAN YOU FEAR IT

When I was nineteen, my college boyfriend (now my husband) invited me on a sailing trip with him and his family. Sounds romantic, right?

Wrong: I am deathly afraid of boats. I'd had only one experience with boats at that point in my life, and it had *not* been a good one.

In the days after he asked me to go sailing, I was an absolute mess. I couldn't stop reliving my experience as a kid, and I even had a series of nightmares about drowning. I didn't know how I could possibly get through another experience of feeling trapped on a boat that could sink at any moment.

But then I had another thought: I truly didn't want to miss out on spending time with this guy I really loved. Especially doing something that *he* loved to do, something that was important to him. If that meant I had to spend a week on a boat, then so be it.

So I went.

And you know what? It wasn't so bad. The weather was perfect, and once I was able to put the months of pre-trip angst aside, I discovered that I was actually enjoying the experience. I didn't drown, get eaten by a shark, or get seasick. In fact, I had fun.

Fear can be tricky that way. It can pop up in your life and make you feel terrible, even when you know your feelings are completely illogical. It can come back to haunt you, even when you believed you had gotten past it. It can come out of nowhere in a giant wave, or it can create a subtle feeling of dread that you have to live with for a long time.

So, what can we do about our fears, especially the ones with so much potential for getting in our way?

The first thing we can do is acknowledge the role fear plays in our lives—in our hopes and dreams, plans for the future, and sense of self. And the second is to decide which is stronger: the fear we're feeling, or the love that's possible on the other side.

I have to admit, I'm still battling my fear of boats. I haven't managed to conquer that one entirely, but I have found the determination within myself not to let it hold me back. And since that cute guy I went sailing with is now my husband and the father of our four children, I'm thankful every day that I went on that trip. Who knows how things would have turned out if I hadn't?

I believe that one of the keys to greatness is personal growth, even when that growth feels awkward. To grow, you have to embrace the discomfort, the awkwardness, and the unfamiliarity. You're out of your comfort zone, which can be really unpleasant, but staying there will cap your potential. You grow your greatness by exploring and expanding your capabilities. You grow by boldly seeking out those Opportunity Jumps whenever you can. Seth Godin says, "Discomfort brings engagement and change. Discomfort means you're doing something that others were unlikely to do, because they're hiding out in the comfortable zone."

And he's right.

The other day, someone asked me to tell them about a specific time in my career when I felt afraid and had to overcome that fear. I struggled to answer because I genuinely couldn't think of a time when I *wasn't* scared out of my mind.

I'm scared. You're scared. We're all scared. And in my opinion the key isn't to eliminate our fears, but rather to learn how to face them and move forward despite them.

My true passion in life is to inspire, motivate, and mentor others to achieve their dreams. It's why I became an angel investor; I love innovation, I love creation, and I love spending time with entrepreneurs. Even though I'm a very private person, I've found that sharing my personal stories of success and failure publicly has helped other entrepreneurs feel less alone. It felt unnatural to share my failures on social media and to talk about the challenges I've faced on TV and relive them in front of thousands of viewers. It felt terrifying to open my life up to the criticism of strangers.

When I began, it was completely out of my comfort zone. Was I doing it right? What would people think? I'd post something on LinkedIn, Instagram, Facebook, TikTok, or Twitter and I would immediately want to delete it. But I didn't. Because, ultimately, I love helping entrepreneurs more than I fear being ridiculed, judged, or rejected online. If I'm able to help just one person, getting criticized doesn't matter.

When I started my first company, I was terrified. I was afraid of failing. I was afraid I didn't know how to be an entrepreneur. I was afraid I would let people down, get rejected, get laughed at . . . you name it, I was scared of it. What I learned after starting was when you're chasing big dreams and trying new things, fear is inevitable. I learned to become the kind of person who faces her fears instead of running away from them.

Whether you're starting a new company, getting on a boat, or broadcasting your past failures publicly, fear is inevitable.

To help me overcome my own fears, I created a simple four-step FEAR process:

1. Feel.

2. Embrace.

3. Act.

4. Repeat.

Step 1: Feel Your Fear

Fear is a survival instinct inherited from early humankind. It is a signal that something is wrong that protects you from danger and allows you to survive. The problem is that your mind often doesn't know the difference between an existential threat—such as a saber-toothed tiger who is about to attack you—and a non-existential threat, like the fear of being embarrassed or rejected on social media. To your mind, it's all the same. Something is wrong. There is a threat to your safety, and you feel scared.

Fortunately, fear is fleeting. Research shows that most emotions only last up to ninety seconds, and that any feeling that lasts longer does so because we've chosen to stay in an emotional loop.[17] So when you feel the fear—especially when you know there's no real existential threat—you may want to remind yourself that it's just a feeling. Your safety is not at risk, and neither is your existence.

Denying your fears will only allow them to have more power over you. Let yourself feel your fear instead of pushing it away or avoiding it, and observe what being afraid feels like. You'll find a power in looking your fear straight in the eye.

Step 2: Embrace Your Fear

Once you feel the fear, you need to embrace it. Why? Because fear is your friend. Remember, the feeling of fear is hardwired into us. It is there to protect us. Once you embrace that fear and accept that it will *always* be present in some form, you can stop wasting time trying to "overcome" or "get rid" of it and start spending time learning how to understand, manage, and work through it.

You can also share your fear. Things are much scarier on the inside than they are on the outside! Shine a bright light on your fear and bring it out of your subconscious and into the forefront. Talk about it with a friend, or write about it in a journal. Once you identify your fear and embrace it, you're that much closer to owning it. Then you can move on to my favorite step: act.

Step 3: Act on Your Fear

Too often, we let our anxiety and insecurities overwhelm us until we're totally paralyzed and can't do anything at all. The most powerful way to overcome fear is to act. Action creates action; momentum creates momentum. So, once you take one step, you'll start building the confidence and the courage to take the next (just like jumping!). Remember, sometimes the risk of *not taking* action is actually greater than the risk of taking a step forward. What would happen if you did nothing? Think about what the outcome would look like three, six, or twelve months from now. Is that outcome greater than the risk associated with jumping in and building the life of your dreams?

Step 4: Repeat

This isn't a process to eliminate your fears, but a process to become a person who faces his or her fears instead of running away from them. The secret is to learn how to turn your fears into your fuel for success. And that takes practice. To make peace with your fears, you need to repeat this process again and again.

Personally, I'd always rather tackle an ocean of fear than a mountain of regret. Every single time you face a challenge or do something unfamiliar, it's going to be a little scary. You will continue to encounter fear, but by feeling it, embracing it, and acting on it, the fear will lose its intensity. Little by little, you'll become stronger than your fears until they no longer have the same kind of power over you that they used to.

At its core, discomfort is about fear. We feel uneasy and agitated because we're afraid we'll get laughed at, that we'll run out of money, that we'll try and try and try and *still* fall flat on our faces.

And honestly? Sometimes we have to listen to those fears. If they're so huge and overwhelming that you can't make an inch of progress without panicking, that's meaningful. If just thinking about your jump makes you totally nauseous or brings you to the brink of tears, that's telling. Trust your gut. You know what's best for you.

But if the discomfort is tied to medium-sized doubts instead of supersized fears, it's worth examining. Poke at it. Name it. Find out where that discomfort comes from and why it's preventing your jump. See if you can use it for fuel instead of allowing it to paralyze you.

Then think about the best possible outcome. Envision yourself, post-jump, enjoying your joy-filled, rewarding, exciting new life. And ask yourself this: Do you want that future more than you dread the minor failures along the way? Do you love it more than you fear it?

If so, keep going. You're on the right track.

Chapter 3 Jump Prep

- Which of the fears is preventing you from jumping? Is it fear of failure, uncertainty, rejection, or not being good enough? You might be facing one, two, or several of these fears. Take a moment to identify which one is holding you back and what strategy you can use to move forward.

- Pinpoint the source of your discomfort by doing the exercise on page 60.

Chapter 3 Jump Hacks

- Practice getting rejected! Ask for a discount at your favorite restaurant for being a loyal customer. Ask to cut in line. Ask for a breath mint. Ask for a sample of something: a piece of salami or a slice of bread. Or if you feel ready to start inching toward your actual jump, take your idea and pitch it to someone you *know* doesn't care or doesn't want it. Practicing potential rejection has two possible outcomes: you're gonna learn, or you're gonna succeed. Either is a win, in my book!

- Start using my simple four-step FEAR process for embracing your fear whenever you feel the emotion rise up. Again, this is something you need to practice, so getting used to the system before your jump will make it easier to apply during and after.

CHAPTER

4

THE POWER OF
DECISION-MAKING

Imagine a world without Netflix.

Okay, wait. That's too scary.

Imagine a world where Netflix never made the transition from a DVD rental service, like Blockbuster, to a world-class streaming service and entertainment empire. It may be hard to process this fact now, but Netflix almost clung to its original business model. That would mean no *Stranger Things*, *Ozark*, or *Bridgerton*. No binge-watching! No instant access to thousands of movies, seasons of shows, and plenty of excuses to procrastinate.

The company's DVD rental-by-mail model was booming in 1999 when founder Reed Hastings chose to completely switch gears. He predicted that, very soon, people would want access to videos on demand, and he began moving Netflix toward providing streaming video via the internet. He did this in the face of *huge* opposition from other company leaders and disbelief from the public. People told Hastings his idea could never be truly profitable. In fact, his cofounder, Marc Randolph, titled his memoir *That Will Never Work* in honor of the discouraging phrase the two founders heard on a near-daily basis![1] People predicted the demise of Netflix so publicly and so often that Hastings literally said, "We've gotten used to it."[2] He was so far ahead of the curve that his decision looked like lunacy at the time.

But now, when the company is raking in more than $20 billion in revenue each year,[3] it is obvious that he made the right choice.

Hastings could've stuck to mailing those DVDs to his customer base and ridden out the success of that model until it collapsed. Instead, he took a visionary Opportunity Jump. He researched consumer preferences and tech trends, then pivoted his company to avoid stagnation. By taking this jump, he pioneered and revolutionized the entire entertainment streaming industry.

You don't need to have Reed Hastings–level decision-making skills to take your jump, but you do need to know the difference between a visionary choice and a wild guess. You've got to know when to seek input from other people and when to listen to your gut. Do the research and identify the risks. Learn to have confidence in your choices. Of course, even the best decision won't yield the best outcome every time. Our decisions aren't made in a vacuum: they're impacted by luck, by other people, and by information we don't have or cannot see. So, even if we feel sure of ourselves, things can still go sideways. We can make a choice that is unquestionably sound and still end up with disappointing results.

Sounds like an argument for avoiding decisions at all costs, doesn't it?

It's not.

It's my way of telling you that *how* you make decisions is as important as the decisions themselves.

THE ART OF CALCULATED RISK-TAKING

Since you can't predict or prepare for all outcomes—and since undesirable results are always a possibility—you've got to learn to make informed choices using incomplete information. It sounds hard, and it is, but it's definitely not impossible. A great place to find lots of experts at this style of partially informed decision-making and risk-taking is the world of poker.

World Series of Poker champion Annie Duke insists that the key to success is to think in "bets," just as you would while playing a game of five-card stud. She says you need to consider how sure you feel about a decision and have a solid understanding of which actions have the highest probability of success. But she also emphasizes that uncertainty is impossible to escape, and that we can't have all the information about . . . well, anything.[4]

But that's the beauty of poker. It's a game of incomplete information by its very nature! Every decision is a calculated risk. And the best players are experts at making smart choices without seeing anyone else's cards. They gather up as many facts and educated guesses as possible by observing the cards in play, the cards they hold, and the actions of the other players. They do their best to gauge the risks and rewards and place bets based on their (incomplete) assessment of the situation. Bets are a great way to mentally frame our non-poker decisions for two key reasons:

1. They help us remember that we can't possibly know everything before we make a choice, *and that's okay.*

2. They help us gauge our levels of certainty.

"A bet is an accountability mechanism," Duke insists. "Imagine that . . . I pin you down on any opinion, and say, . . . 'Do you want to bet your life on that opinion?' . . . I doubt that you would say yes. You would realize that whatever that belief that you have . . . can't be 100 percent."[5]

Wanna know how sure you are about a choice? Ask yourself if you'd bet your life on making the right call. That brings everything into focus in seconds flat, doesn't it?

As you begin to make decisions leading up to your jump, try to think like a poker player. Take facts where you can get them, make assumptions based on careful observation, and place bets based on your incomplete view with your best hunch of the situation. You aren't guaranteed to win (or lose) every time, but you'll hone your skill at making the best decisions you possibly can.

AVOID INFORMATION OVERLOAD

"Analysis paralysis" is *most* likely to attack when you're wrestling with concrete decisions. As you gear up for your transformational jump, you may hesitate while you imagine the million ways your plans could unfold . . . but when it comes to deciding if you should move to Seattle or San Diego? Choosing if you should study film at NYU or UCLA? Picking a storefront location for the boutique of your dreams, settling on a producer to bring your debut album to life, or deciding which angel investors to pitch to? This is when you need to prevent yourself from researching and fact-finding for too long.

Here are some reasons to avoid overanalysis:

You'll Stop Listening to Your Gut

I'm obviously not advocating for snap decisions across the board. But there are two huge reasons why making the occasional choice based on gut instinct is beneficial:

1. Multiple studies have shown that intuition can be more useful than deliberation in some cases. I read about a professor at the Johns Hopkins Carey Business School who did a simple experiment that illustrates this beautifully: He quizzed German and US students to see if they could guess which city was larger: Detroit or Milwaukee. The Germans were 90 percent correct that Detroit is bigger, while the Americans were only 60 percent correct. Why did this happen? "Because the Germans simply picked the one they'd heard more about and guessed it was the larger of the two. Americans, armed with 'knowledge' of these cities, didn't reach for the obvious—and failed."[6] Go with your first instinct, and win. Indulge in self-questioning and self-doubt, and lose.

2. Possibly more important is *the story you're telling yourself* by dismissing your gut. If you never make a decision based on instinct alone, you're declaring, "I don't trust my own observations. I'm not smart or capable enough to just follow my intuition. I need facts or opinions from some other source of confirmation before I can take action." That's negative self-talk. It's a slow but effective way to wear down your self-confidence and make yourself feel incompetent.

You'll End Up with More Data Than You Can Vet

If you indulge your urge to google everything, you may end up with a mountain of data. Some of it will be inaccurate or irrelevant, but you may never be able to sort through it and find out because there will be so. Much. Of. It. You'll be overwhelmed and unable to put all that raw information to use. Which means you will have wasted your time and energy.

You Won't Get the Clarity You Seek

There's no denying that asking questions and investigating options creates a more detailed picture of a situation, but detail isn't always what we need to make the right choice. By adding more variables and scenarios to a decision, we may make the choice harder instead of easier. Time and analysis have value in the decision-making process, but they don't always bring clarity.

Sometimes overanalysis impedes your ability to trust your gut. This is especially true when the jump you're planning involves other people. I experienced this type of "paralysis" when I was thirty-two and my company needed an immediate cash influx. If we didn't get the funding, we wouldn't make payroll, and the business would go bankrupt. I asked our investors for more money, but they were hesitant about putting in any additional capital. I was so confident in my gut that my company would be successful, I called some of my closest friends and asked if they wanted to invest . . . but no dice, they laughed at me. So I decided to show them all how certain I was by putting my money where my mouth was: I loaned the company the money myself. And guess what?

After that, the investors matched me. We were hanging on by a thread, and this influx of cash allowed my company to stabilize and put ourselves in a position for growth. Eventually, I sold that company for $235 million dollars.

Major disclaimer: I haven't always listened to my gut, and I regret that. Sometimes I've made mistakes because I trusted my mind over my gut, rationalizing a bad choice because I wanted or needed it to work. I've done this many times, often around hiring new people. I needed to fill a position, the résumé looked great, the references checked out, but something in the pit of my stomach told me the hire could be a problem. My intuition was trying to get my attention. My mom has always told me that "maybe means no," but I tried to rationalize the hire based on my immediate needs. I wanted it to work. Have you ever been there? Looking back, I could have avoided making these big mistakes if I would have just trusted my gut.

I've also seen this happen with dating. We usually know instinctively if someone isn't right for us, but we also may ignore the red flags. We often brush aside warning signals so we can see the fantasy we want instead of the reality in front of us. We make excuses: He's just in a bad mood because he's hungry. He had a hard day at work and he's tired. I'm sure she didn't mean that super-offensive joke! Even when our intuition is screaming at us to *run run run*, we stay put. When it comes to people, it's especially important to trust our instincts; our gut knows when the connection isn't a healthy one.

The whole notion of "trusting your gut" has been around for ages, but the fact is that many of us don't know what it means in practice. How will we know what our instincts are telling us to do? What does it *feel like* to trust your gut?

I think about it in terms of which choice gives me butter-flies and which choice leaves me with a pit at the bottom of my stomach. Your body is a compass, so trust your physical reaction. When something feels like the right choice, I feel light, energetic, open, motivated, inspired. When my gut tells me something is wrong, I feel heavy, nauseous, sweaty, stiff, anxious. I've been amazed by how trusting my instincts has helped me make the most successful gut-level choices.

Listening to your gut is something that really works best when you create the space and time to do it. In order to tune into those messages from your intuition and understand how they're being reflected in your body, you need a clear mind, a quiet space, and a moment to breathe. Too much noise or dis-traction will overshadow your gut instincts, and you may not be able to discern what you're really feeling. In order to "check in" with your gut, find a spot that helps you feel relaxed—a cozy room in your house or an outdoor space—and take a few moments to center yourself before you consider your options. *Then* you'll be in a perfect frame of mind to examine your choices and find out which one gives you butterflies . . . and which one creates a pit in your stomach.

If you are the type of person who's prone to information overload or analysis paralysis, I strongly recommend that you practice trusting your intuition. Do this actively and mind-fully in your daily life, starting now. Honing this skill will be especially helpful as you begin making choices around your jump! When you're staring at two or more options (Seattle or San Diego? NYU or UCLA?), resist the temptation to research them into oblivion. Instead, notice how your body feels when you think about the options. How does it feel when you think about choosing Option A? Or choosing Option B? It may not always feel logical, but if one option feels better than the other, it will likely lead to success.

ESCAPE THE WHEN/THEN TRAP

If you're someone who worries about being fully ready and completely prepared to make a decision, you might use the when/then trap as an excuse to procrastinate and avoid action. Many people use when/then as an excuse to stay stagnant: "When _____ finally happens, then I will _____."

- "When I lose five pounds, then I'll be ready to start dating."
- "When the economy gets more stable, then I will be ready to look for a new job."
- "When I retire, then I will pursue my passion."
- "When work calms down, then I'll spend more time with my family."
- "When I have saved up $10,000, then I will launch my own business."

Be wary of creating when/then roadblocks and using them as excuses to postpone your dream. The majority of the time, we create these contingencies because we are scared of taking a jump. As a general rule, stop "rain-checking" on what will make you feel the most fulfilled. Because the truth is, you'll probably look back on this time in your life and wish you would have started sooner.

I've struggled with the when/then trap myself. A few years ago, I was talking to one of my mentors, and I told him, "When I retire, then I'll be ready to write a book." He asked me why

I felt I had to wait to pursue my goal and why I couldn't start writing it now. The simple solution never dawned on me: I could be the CEO of a company *and* still find time to write a book. It was not a when/then situation; it was an instance of "I can do _____ *and* _____."

That conversation forever changed the way I lived my life. It opened my eyes to how much I had been holding myself back because it was easier to tell myself the time wasn't right than to accept that the time was now. When I started thinking about my life goals as trains on parallel tracks instead of trains waiting at the station for the next one to leave, it expanded my view of what I could accomplish.

When I decided to work on my passion projects in parallel to my professional career, it renewed and sparked my energy and creativity in all tracks of my life. I realized I could work on starting a family, writing a book, running a company, and helping other entrepreneurs all at the same time. I'd just be a bit tired.

Like me, you can find ways to keep working on your goals in parallel so you don't have to wait to complete one to start another. Let your experiences unfold in tandem so they can support each other, and decide to start now.

And trust me, you're way more ready than you think you are.

BE 70 PERCENT READY

When I sold my first company, I was 70 percent ready. This sounds crazy, right? Since I'd built the company myself without any investors, I didn't have a business plan or any of the typical financial documentation you need for a big sale. I hadn't built the company with the intention of selling it, I built the company to give myself financial freedom. In fact, selling had never occurred to me until I was having lunch with a friend who said *he* was selling *his* company!

"Really?" I said. "That's amazing! Maybe I could sell mine too."

Our conversation got my gears turning, and I dove into researching what I'd need to make a solid sale. I reverse engineered a business plan. I met with my friend's banker. I had my financials audited by a professional accounting firm. I got all my ducks in a row and made it happen. Even though I'd never sold a company before, I was confident I could do it. I embraced an incredibly intense process with both arms for several reasons.

- I knew I was good at sales in general. If I could sell services or products, why couldn't I sell an entire enterprise?

- I understood that the business I'd built was a good one. A really good one. I knew it inside and out and was fully prepared to explain why it was a fantastic investment for someone else.

- I was comfortable being uncomfortable!

The sale took some time, and it took plenty of resources. I hired an investment banker to run a formal process and made nearly a hundred calls and presentations to potential buyers. I wasn't 100 percent ready, but I knew I didn't need to be. I was ready enough. For someone who didn't have experience selling a company, I learned quickly. Eventually, we received seven offers and ended up selling to a European advertising company. I made many mistakes throughout the process, but I was able to take the learned lessons and apply them to selling my next company and the companies I invested in thereafter.

For many people, confidence is linked to readiness. The more ready they feel, the more confident they become. I'm all for doing your research and exploring your options, practicing your curveball until it's unhittable and practicing your speech until it's unforgettable. Preparation is vital, but it's also different from readiness. Preparation has to do with understanding the facts and risks; readiness is about how you *feel*. I've come to believe that there's no such thing as being truly and fully "ready" and no reason to wait until you know every angle, factor, detail, and possible hiccup before taking action.

In my experience, being 70 percent ready is plenty, and I'm not alone in thinking this way. Former US secretary of state Colin Powell is a big fan of the 40–70 rule, which says that you need no less than 40 percent and *no more* than 70 percent of the available information to make a good choice. Surprising, right? Which is why advocates of the 40–70 rule say that when you're obsessed with finding more than 70 percent of the data, you're wasting time. Your window of opportunity will close, and the competition can capitalize on your hesitation.[7]

Even when it comes to pitching a multimillion-dollar idea to investors, it's impossible to be 100 percent ready. Entrepreneurship always involves a high amount of risk, and you can't predict or prepare for every outcome. You'll have to learn to make informed decisions using incomplete information. You need to get comfortable reading the room so you understand who needs the most convincing and who you need to sell. You might also benefit from interacting with your audience and adjusting on the fly so you can articulate what they need to hear. In a meeting, a perfectly reasonable response is, "We're still exploring that and will get back to you." Of course this does *not* apply to memorizing your lines for a play, mixing dangerous chemicals, building a bridge, or skydiving. Some things require 100 percent certainty.

But starting a side business? Becoming a freelancer? Adopting a puppy? Changing careers at age fifty? Seventy percent prepared is plenty. In fact, it would be hard to push past 70 percent without a crystal ball: there's no way to predict everything that might happen, so there's no way to reasonably prepare for every possible scenario.

Another reason to live by the 40–70 rule: room for improvisation is *so* important! When you overplan and overprepare, you're locking yourself into a single possible path. When you give yourself wiggle room, your path might fork and lead you in a new—and *even better*—direction.

Here's the catch: You can only show up 70 percent ready if you are 100 percent confident in yourself. If you're comfortable being uncomfortable and able to improvise. If you understand the facts and the risks and trust yourself to navigate them. Comedian and writer Tina Fey has famously said, "Say yes and you'll figure it out afterward."[8] *That's* the attitude you need to make "70 percent ready" work for you: the conviction to say yes, and the self-confidence to puzzle it all out once the deal is sealed.

DECISIONS ARE BEGINNINGS, NOT ENDINGS

Let me tell you a secret: you can change your mind.

The choices you make are almost never permanent. Life is fluid, and going with Option A now doesn't mean Option

B is off the table for the rest of your life. Just because you decide to pick UCLA for film school doesn't mean that, three semesters in, you can't transfer to NYU. Just because you got a degree in law doesn't mean you can't change career paths and become an artist. Just because I've spent the last fifteen years building my career and life in San Diego doesn't mean I can't pick up and start over in Miami. Making a decision doesn't preclude a pivot.

Choose now knowing that you can choose again later.

When I started my first company, my vision was to build a business and be in control of my own destiny. I was emotionally and mentally exhausted from my previous job, and I wanted to start over on my own terms. I wanted to build a profitable business where I called the shots. I didn't build it to sell it, and I never dreamed it would become as large as it did. We doubled revenue year over year, and what started as a startup grew to a big business with an office, employees, and its own set of challenges. I would sleep with a pager (yes, a pager) and get alerted if there was a tech issue at all times of the night. Ultimately, I decided to sell it to a larger European buyer that had the expertise, infrastructure, and capital needed to sustain our continuous growth.

I did not make this decision because I was fed up with the company I'd built myself, totally from scratch. I did it because I was ready for a change and a new challenge. This decision was the beginning of an entirely new adventure. Yes, I got cash, but I also got to spend the next five years working around the world, meeting brilliant people, and building my network. From Paris to Milan, Amsterdam to London, and Munich to Madrid, I was able to expand my whole world in marvelous and unexpected ways.

The choices you make leading up to your jump are important, but they're not irreversible. Your jump is just the next
chapter in your life, not the final one! If you've struggled with
making tough choices and being decisive, try to remember
that you can always pivot. You can always try something new
or something else.

This jump you're envisioning is going to rock your world,
and the fact that it has appeared in your mind *and* prompted
you to buy my book means you're ready for a transformative next step. If you struggle to make and trust your decisions because you fear other people's criticism, you are not
alone. If you have friends or family members who are guaranteed to nitpick your idea or question your dream, you're
in good company. If you aren't concerned about the people
close to you but worry that investors or banks or even jerks
with active Reddit accounts will laugh at you, I completely
understand.

But you can't let them stop you.

When I started my first business from Hawaii, people I
loved and trusted told me I was crazy. They warned me that
the internet was a fad, that the digital advertising market was
weak, and that I should stay where I had more opportunities.
I can remember having dinner with some of my friends the
night before I uprooted my life and moved to Hawaii. When
we hugged goodbye they said, "Enjoy your vacation!" Before
that moment, I didn't know a hug could feel like a slap in the
face! This wasn't a vacation. I was going to Hawaii so I could
live in my boyfriend's apartment rent-free and save every
penny I had to build the company. It stung. They obviously
didn't believe in me or my idea. But I had confidence in my
decision, and I went anyway.

The people who will try to hold you back will have a million different reasons for doing so. Some will think they're
protecting you; some will be jealous; some will believe they're
helping you refine your vision so you have a better shot at
success. Their motivations don't really matter. Unless you've
asked for their help and input, you can tune them right out.
This is your vision, your idea, your jump to take. Doing it will
make you and other people uncomfortable because change
makes people uncomfortable.

But change is what fuels creativity, passion, learning, innovation . . . *life*. And just as you can't let yourself stay comfortable and unchanged for decades at a time, you can't be
responsible for making everyone around you comfortable
with *your* decisions. You're going to change, and it's going
to make them nervous or judgy or nosy. You don't have to
manage that. You just have to continue making decisions,
continue moving forward, continue preparing for that jump.

You just have to love it more than you fear it.

You just have to trust yourself.

And you are learning to do that right now.

Chapter 4 Jump Prep

- Practice trusting your gut with small choices. Focus on the feeling—do the choices give you butterflies or leave a pit in your stomach? Trust your physical reaction.

- Identify which of the strategies you've read about will help you from over-researching and overanalyzing as you prepare to make pre-jump decisions. Is it being 70 percent ready? Taking a calculated risk? Escaping the when/then trap?

Chapter 4 Jump Hacks

- Identify an area in your life where you can practice being 70 percent ready. Make it something small and manageable, something that won't have too much of an impact but where you can get comfortable being uncomfortable. (This one is especially vital for all you perfectionists out there!)

- Another way to force yourself to trust your instincts on a smaller scale is to count to ten, then make a decision. Don't do this with buying a new car or adopting a pet! Start small: Where are you going to dinner? What color should you paint your bedroom? Are you ready to present your idea to your boss? Give yourself ten seconds—be still, close your eyes, listen to your gut feeling —then decide!

- Practice saying no to prioritize your time. As you approach your jump, you may need to spend more and more of your free time planning and prepping. By carving out some of that time now, you are making the choice to prioritize yourself and your goals. You are deciding to actively make room in your life and schedule for what's to come. It's a great way to build your skills as a confident decision-maker.

- Studies have proven that microdecisions make bigger decisions easier, so practice making small choices leading up to large ones. Let's go back to an example from earlier in the chapter: Say you're settling on a producer to bring your debut album to life. That's the macro decision. Micro decisions could include questions like, What is your price range? How quickly do you want to get the album done, and which producers have availability during that time? Do you need someone who has experience working with beginners? Do you need someone who can help you find additional musicians? Answer these questions and make the associated choices, and *then* narrow down your list of producers based on the ones who fit the bill!

CHAPTER

5

DEFINE SUCCESS ON
YOUR OWN TERMS

*When you're three years old, not peeing your pants is
success.*
*When you're six years old, not getting ketchup all over your
clothes is success.*
When you're twelve years old, passing algebra is success.
*When you're twenty-four years old, having your own apart-
ment is success.*
When you're fifty years old, not balding is success.
When you're sixty-five years old, retiring is success.
*When you're ninety-five years old, not peeing your pants is
success.*

Success is relative, personal, and always changing. And
as your life continues, you'll keep defining and redefining
success in different ways. Money and prestige are two of the
most traditional markers of success, and they both have their
advantages, but there's a lot more to defining success than
bank accounts and fancy titles.

Many of us mistakenly believe that success is always
about work. But this simply isn't true. Success can be defined

in infinite ways. Success for you can be freedom, it can be health, it can be joy. Success can be the ability to spend more time with your family.

Leading tech entrepreneur and Reddit cofounder Alexis Ohanian has been a critical voice in reframing how people view success for modern men. After his wife, Serena Williams, one of the best tennis players in the world, nearly died during childbirth, she was bed-bound for the first six weeks of their daughter's life . . . leaving Alexis as the primary caregiver. He'd never even held a baby before!

Since then, Alexis has been a vocal advocate for parental leave and striving to change how people everywhere view fatherhood. Reddit offers both parents sixteen weeks of paid parental leave, a benefit that many employers do not offer.

The unfortunate reality is that even when companies do offer it, men can feel uncomfortable accessing the benefit as it is not yet a cultural norm, especially for senior executives. Alexis is leading a social shift in how male success is presented and measured so it includes both career and family.

"These things are not mutually exclusive," he says. "A man can be just as career-driven, just as passionate, just as effective whether or not he takes time off to be with his family when welcoming a new child."[1]

Another great example of someone who defines success on his own terms is Rubin Ritter. Rubin was the forum chief executive of the online fashion retailer Zalando, and he helped turn the German-based startup into one of the world's top online fashion retailers, with fourteen hundred employees. At the height of his career and company success, with more than two years left on his contract as CEO, Ritter announced publicly he was stepping down to focus on his family, saying his wife's career should "take priority" in the coming years. "I want to devote more time to my growing family," he shared. "My wife and I have agreed that for the coming years, her professional ambitions should take priority." Ritter reflected on the decision to leave, saying, "I feel that it is time to give my life a new direction."[2] He chose to define his success differently, leaving a financially successful and powerful position at the young age of thirty-eight to prioritize his family and his wife's career—and make a jump!

Personally, I define success more broadly, and my definition always encompasses four areas: physical, emotional, spiritual, and financial. Make sure to measure your success by your own standards and not by society's. This will not be easy to do, and it can be challenging when the world puts so much emphasis on financial success. When someone tells me they are really successful, I always ask, "In what areas?" I believe success is much bigger than a bank account, and I try to encourage others to expand their definition too. Here's how a few of the most influential leaders and thinkers have defined success over the years:

Maya Angelou: "Success is liking yourself, liking what you do, and liking how you do it."

Arianna Huffington: "A third measure of success that goes beyond the two metrics of money and power, and consists of four pillars: well-being, wisdom, wonder, and giving."

Oprah Winfrey: "There is nothing more powerful than you using your personality to serve the calling of yourself."[3]

Richard Branson: "I know I'm fortunate to live an extraordinary life, and that most people would assume my business success, and the wealth that comes with it, have brought me happiness. But they haven't; in fact, it's the reverse. I am successful, wealthy, and connected because I am happy."

Me: I define success by the number of lives I can positively impact. I love supporting entrepreneurs so they can change the world with their ideas. I love mentoring and coaching, connecting people, and offering resources, anything that enables me to support others in the ways I've been supported throughout my life.

All of these definitions are different, and they're not centered around money. Some are centered on the self, some on other people, a few are about feelings, some are about growth . . . and a quick Google search will show you that dozens of accomplished people have defined success in yet more ways. Because the simple truth is that the definition of success is the most personal thing there is.

And that's good!

It means there is no single "right" way to define success. It means that everyone views success differently, so everyone gets to decide for themselves when they've achieved it. Including *you*.

CLARIFY WHAT YOU WANT

Since success can be framed any way you want, you should decide what it looks like to you. It's crucial to do this before you begin planning for or taking your jump since it can influence your process, benchmarks, and ultimate results. This jump is all about your goals and needs, so take some time to formalize how you want to see it play out.

Start by asking yourself, "What do I really care about?" It's a broad question, and you can interpret it based on the specific jump you're planning. Then ask yourself, "What are my core values?" If you are gearing up for a career jump, ask, "What type of work is the most rewarding to me?" or "How do I want to feel when I'm doing my work?"

Then ask yourself, "What impact do I want to have?" Your impact may be on your family, your colleagues, your friend group, your community, or some combination of these. And remember, even if it's just one person, that positive impact will have a domino effect and multiply. Here are three exercises I use to help me define what success means to me before I jump.

Defining Success Exercise 1: Components of Success

Success is very rarely just one thing. You can have enormous power over a small group of people and still not feel successful. You can even have lots of money, awards, and accomplishments and still feel unfulfilled. So start by imagining yourself *after* your jump, feeling satisfied, proud, and, yes, successful. What are the components of that feeling? Are they all internal, or do they involve the opinions of other people?

In this post-jump scenario, are you no longer worried about something that's plagued you your whole life (like debt, criticism, even some aspect of your appearance)? Your personal components of success may include satisfaction, abundance, recognition, feelings, relationships, security, the removal of barriers, and (of course) the classics like money and power!

Defining Success Exercise 2: Understanding Goals and Visualizing Dreams

In my opinion, goals are concrete and dreams are hazy. The jump that you're planning to take soon is likely a goal: it's a change you'll make or an action you'll take with a specific set of results in mind. But that jump/goal is likely to be part of a larger dream you have for yourself, a long-term vision that can only be achieved with years of planning and work. For example, let's say the jump you're planning is to launch your own IT consulting business. That's a goal since it's got one discrete end result: the business itself. But your *dream* might be to own a chain of IT consulting firms all across the country that help small or women-owned businesses handle internal operations. Or it might be to become an IT thought leader who writes and speaks about how technology can improve our world. See how the goal and dream are on different levels? With that in mind, consider your own goals, think about how they feed into your dreams, and try to write down a few notes about what success would look and feel like at *both* levels. (By the way, thinking back to when I started my first company, I wish I could tell myself to dream bigger. While caution can keep you from making harmful mistakes, it can also stop you from reaching your full potential. Allow yourself to dream bigger and reach for greater success.)

Defining Success Exercise 3: Outputs Versus Outcomes

Just as goals and dreams operate on two different levels, so do outputs and outcomes. Say you have an amazing idea for a screenplay and want to turn it into a movie. The movie itself would be the output: it's a single project that gets completed and results in the creation of a product or body of knowledge. Becoming a respected and beloved screenwriter is an outcome: it's a consequence of the work you did, and it encompasses your transformation as a person. Neither of these is better than the other. Your definition of success can definitely include outputs, especially if you love creating or inventing. But as you ponder, think about how you want to change as a person and what outcomes you might strive for. When you picture the most successful version of yourself, is that person skilled, funny, fearless, beloved, or innovative? What traits or abilities has your successful self gained as *outcomes* from his or her work, studies, experiences, or creative endeavors?

After completing these three exercises, you will have a precise and detailed definition of personal success. Once you have that, I recommend paying more attention to what you *do* in your daily life. If you define success by a certain variable but don't put any energy toward it, is it really a priority? Or are you lying to yourself? If you discover you've cooked up a definition that doesn't truly align with who you are, that's okay! Go back and revise. You're a work in progress, and so is this definition. You'll get more and more honest with yourself as you learn and grow.

WHAT SUCCESS "SHOULD" LOOK LIKE

Even after defining success for yourself, you may waver. When the people in your life learn about your jump, they may try to impose their own ideas about success on you. You will undoubtedly see portrayals of success in the news and other media that focus exclusively on money and fame, and these shared ideas about what a full, rich life "should" be may cause you to question your custom-made definition.

That's fine. None of us are immune to outside influences. But I urge you to push back when these forces start to creep in.

Who's to tell you what you should do? Who says you should get married, you should hold down a nine-to-five job, you should have a child, you should retire, you should look a certain way or spend your energy on certain goals? The list of "you shoulds" is almost endless, and that makes it daunting. But "you shoulds" aren't about you; they're about someone else's definition of success.

There may be a gap between what you actually want and what your parents, friends, or coworkers think you *should* want. You need to honor that, and accept that your own vision for yourself is authentic and worth protecting. Once you stop listening to the clamor of other voices and opinions, you'll be free to pursue the things that matter most to you (not to everyone else). When I hear the word *should*, I stop and ask myself, *Whose voice is that? Is it one of my parents', is it society's, is it the industry's, or is it really* my voice? Be sure your definition of success is defined by you.

With that in mind, it's time to decide how you're going to measure your progress. The definition you've written for yourself will give you the parameters you need to envision the finish line, but you'll still need to hone in on some mile markers. You also need to get specific about what crossing that finish line means to you.

MEASURE WHAT MATTERS

By this point, you should have two things fully fleshed out:

1. A clear picture of what you want to achieve (your vision)

2. Your personal definition of success

These building blocks will be the foundation that supports you before and after your jump. They will *also* help you understand how to measure what matters and ignore what doesn't. Your vision may involve starting a business, switching careers, going to school, buying a home, or asking for a raise. Whatever it is, it needs to be personally motivating enough for you to want to commit to achieving it.

How will you know when it's achieved, especially in light of what you now know about outcomes versus outputs? Even if your jump revolves around starting a business, will you consider yourself a success once the business is launched? Or do you need to have earned a certain amount of revenue first? Or served customers for a particular length of time?

The jump itself is just one element of the overall success you desire, and in order to enjoy that success as fully as possible, you may want to create some metrics for yourself.

In a business context, metrics are things like profitability and growth: concrete measurements that show positive trends. In life, metrics may revolve around how content, healthy, or engaged you feel. Since your jump is likely to have overlap between work/achievement and life/feelings, you should consider drawing metrics from both categories. Here are a few examples to get the brainstorm started:

METRICS FOR WORK/ ACHIEVEMENT	METRICS FOR LIFE/FEELINGS
Creation of a new company or endeavor, marked by a launch date	Pride in accomplishments, to the point that I want to share the news with people in my life
$10,000 in revenue	A sense of financial security / worrying less about money matters
Six months in business	I spend more of my time doing things I enjoy than things I dread
A promotion with a raise and more responsibility	Feeling valued and fulfilled by my work and daily activities

Think about what you're hoping to change or accomplish with your jump, and then list out some possible metrics so you can track your progress. If it would help motivate you, add some reminders to consider your metrics to your calendar. This can just mean sitting down for ten minutes at the beginning of the day and checking in with yourself. Take note of anything concrete like earnings or tasks that have been checked off your to-do list, but also reflect on your emotional state. If one of your life/feelings metrics is "less stress in my family relationships," consider how you feel now in comparison to how you felt a week or a month ago. Have you made progress? If not, what should you change?

As you consider metrics and measurement, be careful about setting up unreasonable expectations for yourself. The idea here is to help you understand your progress and make adjustments as needed . . . *not* to make you feel disheartened for moving too slowly! On a related note, don't let anyone else tell you what your metrics should be. "Measure what matters" means finding ways to chart and check on the signs of progress that matter to *you* and only you. The only reason to track your journey toward success at all is to boost your motivation. So pick measurements that resonate with you, align with your values, and help you stay happily on track.

MAKE PEACE WITH THE PAST

In the next chapter you'll dive into creating your one-year success plan. Before you do that, it's a good idea to pause and take stock of what you're about to leave behind. You can't completely change your future without finding resolution in your past. This can be challenging work, but it's essential to growth. I've had to do it myself several times, and it's helped me commit to my own jumps as well as learning how to support others who are preparing to jump.

In my experience, every time you jump you are one major step closer to something better: a relationship, a job, a city, a dream. But in order to make the most of your jump, you need to fully understand and accept what you're moving away from and why. This is actually the best opportunity to make peace with your past.

Here are a few guiding questions to help you get started:

- *What are you hoping to leave behind?* This can be behav iors, people, mistakes you've made, or anything that you want to stay in the past.

- *What are you hoping to find?* When you jump away, how will your life improve? If it doesn't, how will you cope?

- *What have you learned?* Focus on the lessons you've taken away from this past situation. How have you grown? How has it made you stronger or smarter or more resilient?

- *How will you carry it?* Dwelling in the past is unhealthy, but so is pretending it didn't happen. What do you want to keep with you? Ideas, feelings, newfound understanding about yourself?

- *How will you let it go?* Making peace with the past is equally about embracing what has happened and releas- ing it. Would it be helpful to perform a ritual to say good- bye to this old part of your life? Or write about it and put the journal on a shelf? Consider how to let go so you can step fully into the present and build a brighter future.

Chapter 5 Jump Prep

- Write down what success means to you. It could be a list, it could be one thing, just make sure it's personal.

- Make peace with your past. What have you already done to make peace with your past? If the answer is "nothing," take some time to identify events or relationships that need some healing and make a plan to address them before you take your jump.

Chapter 5 Jump Hacks

- Jumping away from a situation means leaving people and situations behind you. In order to make peace with them, you'll need to have some tough conversations. After you've spent time with the questions under "Make Peace with the Past," make a list of people you need to meet with before your jump. Sketch out what you need to say, find out, or explain. You can use this template to make these conversations less scary:

Dear [name],
I am preparing to make some big, positive changes in my life, but before I do, I'm working on making peace with my past. I would love to talk with you sometime soon because [issue or incident] stands out in my mind as something unresolved between us. I know it might be a little awkward, but I think it will make us both feel

better in the long run. Can you send me some dates and times that work for you? Thanks for considering this request. You're helping me get closer to an important goal.

[Signature]

CHAPTER

6

CREATE YOUR
ONE-YEAR SUCCESS PLAN

Depending on what you're trying to accomplish, a year can feel like an eternity or a heartbeat. Even when you're just living your life and *not* preparing for a jump, it's a stretch of time that can either fly right by or drag on endlessly. But in my opinion, a year is a useful yardstick for most jumps since it provides you with just enough leeway to prepare yourself and take action, but not so much that you'll end up spinning your wheels. Your one-year success plan will be your secret weapon to navigating this new territory. And trust me: you need a plan! You wouldn't go into a forest without a map, and you shouldn't make a big jump without a plan.

In the world of business, a year is typically considered a very short stretch of time. Corporations think in five-year increments, and even entrepreneurs tend to need more than twelve months to make huge changes. But both entrepreneurs and companies can agree that one year can make a world of difference, especially when motivated. Benjamin Franklin once said, "If you fail to plan, you are planning to fail."

I often think about my friend whose story showcases the power and necessity of a one-year success plan. When he was forced to completely pivot his business during the 2020 pandemic, he created a one-year plan to help him focus on the specific steps necessary to transform his business. Here is his story in his own words:

Our small team was looking at the numbers, and we couldn't believe it. We had just surpassed ten thousand sign-ups in two months for our new social app, and people were actively using it. Investors messaged us letting us know that we'd "nailed it" and that they "loved the mission." Unlike other social networks, which are largely antisocial, our app's purpose was to inspire people to go out into the physical world to connect in person with friends and make new ones. We spent two years building and iterating, trying different approaches, fueled by every entrepreneur's dream that we would catch the elusive lightning in a bottle. In February of 2020, we were finally on our way. One month later, the COVID-19 pandemic forced everyone across the world to stay at home and not socialize in person. Our dream became a nightmare.

With little money left in the bank, we needed to make a decision. Shut down the company, or attempt one last moonshot with a new product? I asked my wife what I should do, and she simply reminded me of the advice I frequently give other entrepreneurs: "Never give up."

A month later, our team pivoted to work on our new product, an online marketplace that makes it easy to connect with world-class experts and get advice over a video call. We naively reached out to some of the most iconic fashion experts and home decorators in the world, hoping that they would join our marketplace. We shared our vision for a better world, where people with dreams could get introductions and advice from experts in their field. Our jump paid off: many of the experts and authority figures in their fields said yes! We worked day and night executing at record speed, designing and building our new product to launch by the end of the year. By December of 2020, we launched our beta, and it was an instant hit. Within one year, I went from the verge of bankruptcy to successfully pivoting the business and raising funds from one of the top VC firms.

I learned a long time ago that those who are willing to adapt are the ones who survive and prosper. For us, what seemed like a blow was really a surprise, and we embraced it by accepting our new path. As Kim puts it, we made the jump . . . and then made the jump again. I'm glad we did.

This is a great example of a company that took a Survival Jump and changed what success looked like for their company in the course of just one year. Imagine what you can achieve if you map out the steps for your jump! You've already started visualizing your destination. Now it's time to plan your route.

YOUR PLAN SHOULD BE ASPIRATIONAL (YET ATTAINABLE)

Before you start planning, researching, or writing, take a breath. In order to create a plan that you'll actually use—one that pushes your boundaries but is also feasible—you need to start with your vision. Good planning begins at the end point, with the goal, and builds backward. Why? Because if you don't know where you're going, you can't expect to get there. So, before you think about what you need to do to get closer to your goal, daily, weekly, and monthly, think about the goal itself.

Create a vision board that shows what your life will be like at the end of these amazing twelve months, after you've jumped and embraced change. Start journaling about the transformations you want to make, and describe them in detail. Or write a news story about who you'll be one year from today. Pick a publication or newsfeed you read daily (*Wall Street Journal*, *USA Today*, etc.) and create a headline that starts with your name and includes details about what you accomplished, what you started, what you invented. (For example, "Kim Perell Funds Three World-Changing Startups Run by Visionary Entrepreneurs.") Then write a mock news story explaining your road to success!

As you dive into the planning process itself, think big … but also keep the plan simple, streamlined, and practical. Believe me when I tell you that overcomplicated plans never work out.

Think about something as commonplace as reducing your social media use. We're all glued to our phones all the time, so plenty of people will give up Instagram for Lent or make a New Year's resolution to reduce their amount of time on Facebook. In fact, you've probably seen someone making an announcement that they're signing off social media for the foreseeable future to spend more time with family, or work on a project, or just give themselves a breather.

And then? Within a month or so, they're back.

I can guarantee that they weren't able to achieve this small, seemingly straightforward goal because they hadn't made any sort of plan to attack it. I'd recommend building a simple plan that creates boundaries for yourself; for example: I will only use social media after work and on the weekends, or I will block social media until my to-do list is complete. Simple plans also work beautifully for higher-commitment goals, like ones that revolve around health and fitness. If you decide to lose fifteen pounds over the next six months but don't give yourself any milestones or guidelines, you'll most likely fail.

The Couch to 5K program is a perfect example of a simple plan that leads to reliable success, and it's one that even works for people who hate running. This nine-week plan was developed by a man named Josh Clark who was *not* a born runner, but who started jogging after a nasty breakup and found that the regular exercise helped him manage his moods.[1] He jotted it down and shared it on his website in 1996, and it has since grown into one of the world's most popular exercise programs.[2] Here's how Couch to 5K works:

- You commit to three runs each week for nine weeks.

- The plan tells you exactly what to do on each run. For the first few weeks, you'll do intervals of walking and running, leading up to all running.

- You can measure your runs by time if you don't have an easy way to measure distance. (Flexibility!)

- The schedule is different each week to keep you on track (and to keep you from getting bored).

That's it. And after nine weeks, you'll be able to run five kilometers! Even if you've never run more than half a block in your life! Clark attributes his program's outstanding success rate to its simplicity and constant delivery of small wins.

"It all starts with being gentle to yourself," he says. "The first week of Couch to 5K asks you to jog for just a minute at a time, an achievable victory for most of us right out of the gate. The challenges gradually increase, but in increments that are always within reach. In the process, one discovers that there's more inside them than they realized."[3]

I love that. This plan is simple, flexible, and has built-in positive reinforcement. It doesn't take a lot of time, and you need absolutely no expertise to get started. Couch to 5K might just be the ultimate foolproof plan.

As you begin to formulate your own plan for the coming twelve months, consider how these elements might fit in. You don't have to have a plan so simple that it can be boiled down to four steps, but you *do* need something that can be explained in a few sentences. You need a plan that can work with your routine, not against it. Consider how you'll build in flexibility and milestones so you can have a few bursts of motivation along the way.

Wondering how to get started? Keep reading for my tips and guidelines for making a truly helpful one-year success plan.

DEVELOPING THE RIGHT PLAN FOR YOU

I'm going to guide you through the process of creating a one-year plan that's simple and flexible—because, as you've already learned, those are the best plans—so you can start taking baby steps toward your eventual jump. Even if you need more than a year to work up to this jump, let's start by planning out those first, crucial twelve months. Then, as you start to see progress, you can adjust your plan or build on it.

My tips for sketching out this plan are a great place to start, but if you're already a plan-making pro, by all means, customize. If, on the other hand, creating a one-year plan makes your palms sweat with anxiety, feel free to use every idea below to get your first draft done, and revisit it when you feel ready.

Capture Your Vision

Your first task is to write down a clear vision on a piece of a paper that includes these three things:

1. Where you want to go in one year

2. What you want to accomplish in one year

3. Who you want to become

This should be like a personal mission statement; it should be passionate but concise, just one paragraph. Whatever form your plan ends up taking, keep this paragraph front and center!

Start Backward

Once you have a clear vision, start working backward, building a framework of milestones you need to hit. What's the second-to-last thing you need to do before you jump? And before that? This reverse engineering process will help you get a sense of how long each step will take and when it will need to be completed. Use whatever tool feels easiest to you: a spreadsheet, a cheap twelve-month calendar, a blank document. I can totally see using a giant sheet of paper and a pencil since I'd undoubtedly need to erase a few steps and move them around!

Set Deadlines

A goal without a deadline is just a daydream. It's got nothing to anchor it to action. Attach due dates and deliverables to everything in this plan, or it won't get done!

Do the Hardest Thing First

Did you know that there's tons of scientific research to support that you make your worst decisions at the end of the day? Conquer your most important task first thing in the morning; this will not only give you a sense of relief for finishing it, but it also gives the rest of your day momentum. As you make your one-year success plan, try to get the most difficult and daunting tasks out of the way as quickly as possible. I do this every day.

Find an Accountability Partner

Even a simple and flexible success plan will be hard to execute at times. Your life is full and busy, your energy is limited, and you're doing something that challenges you! Getting an accountability partner is a great way to keep yourself on track and ensure you follow through with your commitments fully and on time. Choose someone who will ask you the hard questions and hold you responsible to the goals you set for yourself.

Celebrate the Small Wins

Success doesn't happen overnight, and it takes time to achieve a big goal. Throughout my career, I have found that celebrating small wins along the journey was an important way to track incremental progress and keep my team motivated and energized.

When I started my first company, we celebrated everything from hitting monthly revenue targets to specific team accomplishments, like completing a prototype, to the anniversaries and birthdays of each employee. We celebrated so much that the team actually asked me to stop ordering cakes for every celebration, so we pivoted to protein shakes and fruit platters. But no matter what, we still celebrated! To commemorate each achievement, we did everything from going to sporting events, concerts, picnics, and happy hours to holding barbecues in the company parking lot and taking summer Fridays off. One time we even got a money booth! This reinforced our progress and created a culture where people felt appreciated.

If you're not sure how to incorporate milestones into your plan, here's a sample of what a month might look like if your goal was to launch a small, online-only business:

MONTH 1:	
WEEK 1 Tasks: Research establishing an LLC Begin brainstorming business names Goals: Set up an informational interview with someone who works in this industry already What Will Success Look Like? Notes on both tasks Calendar entry for interview Begin setting aside money for LLC filing as needed	**WEEK 3** Tasks: Ask for recommendations for programmers and graphic designers Goals: Choose a name Start brainstorming logo ideas What Will Success Look Like? List of trusted website builders (at least three of each category) Name chosen Continue saving fifty dollars per week
WEEK 2 Tasks: Ask for recommendations for accountants Talk to bank about setting up a business account Goals: Get input on name ideas from trusted friends and colleagues Begin saving fifty dollars per week for initial business costs What Will Success Look Like? List of trusted accountants Narrow down name ideas to top five Begin saving (move to business account when established)	**WEEK 4** Tasks: Send paperwork and payment to state for LLC Buy domain name Goals: Start reaching out to programmers; ask for pricing and availability Start reaching out to graphic designers; ask for pricing and availability What Will Success Look Like? Ideally, have completed your first informational interview by now and possibly set up a second Begin narrowing down web-build team choices Continue saving fifty dollars per week
MONTHLY CELEBRATION:	Happy hour with friends

Your one-year success plan needs to become part of your life and part of your routine. Make sure to incorporate its dates and milestones into your regular calendars and time-trackers. If you spend days writing up this plan and shove it in a drawer, it will never get done. If you put "Set up coffee with industry professionals by February 1" in your phone calendar, you'll remember to hold yourself accountable. Put every single task and milestone in your calendar, and set up reminder notifications so the activities and goals you've meticulously outlined will actually get done. The mini-jumps you take en route to the big one need to happen at regular intervals to ensure progress and build momentum.

So write your plan, and then set dates and reminders in your calendar. Make it real. Make it unavoidable. Trust me: it's the best way to keep yourself on track. You've got this.

SET YOURSELF UP FOR SUCCESS

Goal setting is a powerful process that gives you the motivation and direction you need to achieve success. I like to create SMART goals (goals that are Specific, Measurable, Attainable, Relevant, and Timely) that I can work toward and track my progress on. I have found nothing more powerful than achieving a goal, big or small. It helps you get used to the idea that you have control over your life and that you have the ability to accomplish anything you put your mind to. (Because you do!)

Each night before I go to sleep, I plan for the day ahead. I prioritize and write down the three things I want to accomplish. That way when I get started in the morning, I know exactly what I need to focus on. This can be anything from following up on a deal I'm working on, reaching out to a mentor to schedule a meeting, or sending a birthday message to a friend. Big or small, professional or personal, significant or a little silly, you should always have a few goals you're working toward. If it's a small goal, accomplish it quickly and move on to the next. If you set a larger goal, break the path into small, achievable, realistic steps—ones you can make daily progress on.

A PATH LEADS TO A PATH

I've always been a champion of action over inaction. When I was growing up, my grandfather taught me the importance of having the courage to take a first step, because once you do, the path you're on will eventually lead to another path. It's helped me muster the confidence and courage to take a lot of important jumps in my career. Something that all the successful people I know have in common is that they take *action*. They know there is no wrong first step. Even if the path you start out on leads you to something that doesn't work, that doesn't mean it's the end of your journey. It just means you need to pivot in a new direction. You just have to have the courage to start.

Life is full of unexpected twists and turns. So don't waste your energy trying to predict every possible scenario that *might* happen! This one-year plan is the start of your path. It's the trailhead. Follow it now, and remain open to the paths that may show up along the way. Take your first steps with an eager, optimistic Beginner's Mind, embrace your curiosity, and revel in the newness of the unknown.

By creating a one-year success plan, you are defining your path. It will lead you to another path, and so long as you trust your choices as you walk, you will always find yourself with all the enticing opportunities you'll ever need.

It's important to remember that change is a process, not an event. Even if the jump itself can happen in a single day or a single week, you need to prepare for it beforehand and be ready to embrace your new life afterward. You're a person who is poised to change and grow, and both change and growth tend to take their own sweet time. A path leads to a path, activity follows action, and all of these things unfold organically.

If you're convinced that you can shorten your timeline, by all means give that a try. But there's a reason I named this chapter "Your One-Year Success Plan." A year will whiz by you. If you're working hard and steadily toward a goal that excites you, that time will absolutely fly. It will also give you enough breathing room to test out ideas, try, fail, backtrack, revise, get help, and experiment. A year is not that long. A year is the perfect amount of time to create meaningful change.

And the year you're about to start? It's going to be *amazing*.

To ensure your success, I've created a free one-year success plan template you can download with a step-by-step, month-by-month plan to make it easy for you to stay on track. You can access the plan at www.kimperell.com/jump.

Chapter 6 Jump Prep

- Create your one-year success plan. I recommend setting aside at least four to six hours to complete it. Really get some quality time alone. Ask your spouse to take the kids, head off for a weekend away, or just head to the local coffee shop with headphones in hand. Grab your calendar, and schedule time when you'll complete your plan.

- Make it a point and habit to prioritize completing the hardest tasks of your day first thing in the morning. Notice how you feel at the end of the day. I bet you will feel more productive and less burned out.

Chapter 6 Jump Hacks

- To ensure your success, I've created a free one-year success plan template you can use to make it easy for you to stay on track. You can download the plan at www.kimperell.com/jump.

- At every one of my companies, I used a trick from the book *Mastering the Rockefeller Habits* by Verne Harnish: I asked every team member to pick three goals or milestones for each month and to monitor their progress toward those goals.[4] This is a fantastic way to stay focused while also forcing yourself to acknowledge progress. If you're not ready to begin tackling your one-year success plan just yet, try this hack to keep yourself on track! Set three goals for each month, and check in with yourself at the end of each week to ensure you're making some headway.

- If you struggle to set and conquer goals—even small ones—consider getting an accountability partner. This can be a friend or family member, someone you see in person or interact with online; it just needs to be someone you like, trust, and respect who's willing to help you make measurable progress toward your stated objectives. Accountability partners are fantastic because they add a somewhat unpleasant but undeniably effective motivator: guilt. *No one* enjoys doing the mental gymnastics required to tell someone you didn't do what you promised to do!

CHAPTER

7

THE ART OF
RELATIONSHIP BUILDING

Where would Ben be without Jerry? Procter without Gamble? Jay-Z without Beyoncé? What are the chances that Larry Page could've built Google without collaborator Sergey Brin? Even people who *seem* like solo successes often have a valued partner or talented team supporting them behind the scenes. Barack had Michelle. Even Steve Jobs got his start with collaborator Steve Wozniak.

Nobody is successful alone.

I can honestly say that I wouldn't be where I am today without all the people who have helped and supported me along the way.

Those who know the power of relationships hone their ability to recognize the strengths and talents of other individuals. Everyone needs stellar teammates in their life and career; trust me. That's right: even if *all* of the work you're doing is individual or internal work, you still need support, you need sounding boards, you need cheerleaders, you need truth-tellers and people who can talk you down from the scariest of ledges. We all need teammates to advise us, lift us up, and walk the path alongside us.

If you've ever watched the Oscars, you always hear the winners thanking long lists of people who have helped them get to that point. Often, the lists are so long the "wrap it up" song gets played during their speeches! I've never heard anyone stand behind the podium and say, "I did this alone! I'm so proud of myself for winning this outstanding accomplishment." First of all, that would be tactless beyond belief. But more importantly, it's wildly unlikely. Impossible, even.

World-changing inventions, phenomenal films, successful businesses, political careers . . . they're all made possible by strong support systems. Successful people have mentors and advisors, as well as great teams who help them bring their plans to fruition. Those teams may work entirely behind the scenes, but never doubt they are there, doing the unseen work that makes public accomplishment possible. Everyone needs help as they plan and execute their jumps. Simply put, people need people.

I know this from painful personal experience. One of the biggest mistakes I made early in my career was believing I had to go it alone. After the bankruptcy and after firing all of the friends I had recruited, I felt like a failure and more alone than ever. Since I never, *ever* wanted to be forced to fire my friends again, it took me a long time to hire anyone. As I was building my new company from my kitchen table, I tried to do everything by myself for as long as humanly possible. I figured that if it was just me handling all the work, I was the only one who could get hurt if something went wrong.

But looking back, it was lonely and hard, and I wish I would've harnessed the power of surrounding myself with great people earlier. I worked myself into exhaustion, often doing things that weren't my forte.

I hit the low point at 3:00 a.m. in July of 2003. I was sitting alone in my "office," which was my kitchen, struggling to keep my eyes open, trying to perfect my sales deck for a call I had at 7:00 a.m. I was emotionally and mentally burned out from simultaneously being the CEO, CMO, CFO, and CTO all at once. Responsibilities kept piling up, and I was drowning trying to stay afloat. When I was actually with other people, I had a short fuse, but more often I found myself lonely and exhausted. I finally admitted that I could no longer do it on my own. I made a commitment to myself to hire people with complementary skills. I called my best friend from college, who was a master at writing and sales, and my old controller, who could help manage the finances, and I asked them to join me on my journey. They were both individuals who I trusted and respected. They would ask me tough questions and push back if they didn't agree with me. That was a tall order. That was the beginning of recognizing the importance of a team.

Once I finally *hired them*, it was astonishing how quickly my energy changed. It wasn't just that more work got done, or that the right people were doing it—though that certainly helped—it was that I finally had collaborators. I got to share my excitement with smart, fun people who were just as excited as I was! I got to bounce ideas off employees I trusted. I got to listen to their input and make better decisions because of the insights they shared. And when things got tough, sharing the hardships and overcoming the challenges with my team made them less painful.

This experience reminded me that life really is a team sport. Everything works better when you've got a squad to back you up.

JUMP

Here are three reasons that teamwork is essential to your personal and professional success.

Delegation

You can't be good at everything. No one can! And when you've got a group of people helping you out, you get to delegate tasks to people who do them exceptionally well. You can even delegate things you simply don't like doing! One of the great joys of building a team is dividing and conquering: making sure that tasks are given to people who excel at and enjoy doing them.

Accountability

Do you think that you're going to follow your one-year success plan to the letter without needing any reminders or encouragement? Do you think everything will go exactly as you imagine and that you'll never need to alter your trajectory when you're already rocketing full speed ahead? Of course you don't. Building a team around you will ensure you have accountability buddies to keep you on course and eager ears to listen when you desperately need to bounce an idea off someone you know and trust.

Community

Having a trusted team makes the work easier to do and the wins more enjoyable. You spend the majority of your day at work, so it's important to surround yourself with people you enjoy being around and working with.

Who should be a part of your team? Only you know that, of course, but try to recruit colleagues, friends, and family members who believe in you and believe in your jump. When you spend your time with people who constantly tell you why you can't achieve your dreams, it's very hard to be successful. When you spend your time with people who truly want to see you live out your dreams, everything becomes a thousand times easier. So ask yourself: Do you have the right people in your life? Are they supporting you while also challenging you to grow and learn? Do you have your team lined up and ready to support you before, during, and after your jump? Think about everyone in your life who plays a pivotal part in helping you get from today to tomorrow.

FIND YOUR MENTOR

I've been lucky enough to connect with multiple mentors throughout my career, all of whom have been key advocates on my way to my success. My parents were my first mentors, but over the years I've worked with numerous colleagues and coaches who I relied on for support, advice, and guidance. They have been my unofficial board of advisors for big decisions, both personal and professional, and I can confidently say that mentors have been absolutely crucial to my ongoing personal success. Just as having the right team to help you celebrate makes those celebrations sweeter, having the right person available to you in a crisis can provide helpful perspective and support when you need it the most.

Your jump is going to catapult you into the unknown, so I strongly encourage you to find a mentor. You'll want to connect with someone who has gone through something similar and can advise you as you navigate through this unfamiliar territory. This is especially true if your jump is into a new career path or entrepreneurial role, since studies show that having a mentor can lead to greater career success, including promotions, raises, and increased opportunities.[1] Mentors are a source of motivation and accountability, regardless of how they're supporting you! Check this out: researchers found that people are 40 percent more likely to achieve their goals if they write them down . . . but that number rockets up to 70 percent if goals are shared with a mentor or colleague.[2] In all my personal experience *and* research, I've never found a downside to working with a mentor. Cultivating this relationship can help with everything from academic achievement to building personal confidence to creating a robust professional network.

Of course, finding a mentor takes both tenacity and patience. While you can certainly scope out online mentorship networks or workplace programs, many people prefer to forge the relationship more organically. I think it's best to start by combing through your in-person and online and social networks for people you admire and who also have relevant experiences. If you need help, try asking trusted colleagues for recommendations: explain what you're hoping to achieve and why you are seeking a mentor, and see if they know anyone who might be a good fit.

I believe it's important to seek a mentor who is different from you in a few fundamental ways. You want there to be similarities, of course, but you'll always learn valuable and unexpected lessons from people who are different from you. Perhaps your mentor is from a different part of the world, or he or she is much older, or he or she is a different gender. If you don't seek someone with a few key differences, you'll build an echo chamber that will propagate your excuses instead of propelling your forward. Be strategic as you narrow your search.

Once you've found the right person, actually having the courage to ask him or her can still be a bit nerve-racking. Anjuli Sastry, cofounder of NPR's Women of Color mentorship program, has great advice on approaching a potential mentor, including having an elevator pitch ready, making sure it's the right fit before asking, and mentioning what you like about the person's work, especially if you've never met.[3]

As you begin to spend time with your potential mentor, pay attention to your chemistry. Make sure it's someone you trust and feel comfortable going to when you run into setbacks. Your mentor should be someone you rely on for unbiased, honest advice—the type of advice you may not get from your family and friends. The best mentor should feel like someone who is both a friend and a role model.

Finally, it's important to make sure that, as a mentee, you respect the time that someone else invests in you. Commit yourself to always being the one in the relationship who takes the initiative to follow through and follow up. When I was growing up, my grandfather got my family shirts, mugs, and hats with the acronym *DWYSYWD* printed on them. Backward or forward it stands for the same thing: Do What You Say You Will Do. They're words I live by and that I expect people I mentor to live by too.

EXPAND YOUR NETWORK

Once you've found a great mentor, it's time to start adding other people to your growing team of supporters. And,
believe it or not, some of the people that will be essential to
your jump are probably strangers to you right now. You hav-
en't met them yet, but they can help you . . . just as soon as you
bring them into your network.

Networking is a skill. Building a network is about making
genuine . . . enriching relationships. Giving out a thousand
business cards in a hotel lobby isn't great networking; it's just
a waste of paper. *Networking* is about awkward five-minute
chats that lead nowhere, but *building a network* is about
making genuine, mutually beneficial connections, and then
investing in those connections so they turn into lifelong,
enriching relationships.

The biggest mistake I see entrepreneurs and individuals
make in their careers is relying on surface-level connections.
The best entrepreneurs and executives I know foster genuine
and deep connections with those in their network: they know
their passions, their dogs' names, their kids' names, their life
goals, their fears, and more. They make a point to show the
person that the relationship they have is priceless and that it
really matters to them. In the business world, where so much
is about the "transaction," being someone who genuinely
values relationships sets you apart.

Bestselling author Tim Ferriss has often said that when
it comes to networking, you should go deep rather than
narrow. Instead of making lots of shallow connections with
lots of people, focus on cultivating deep, meaningful relationships with a few key individuals.[4] I completely agree! I'd

add to his advice by saying never underestimate the power and value of being a great, intentional listener. People want to feel heard and understood, so showing genuine curiosity about their interests and lives will forge instant connections. A rule of thumb I use when meeting new people is to spend 80 percent of the time asking questions so I can learn more about them. I ask questions like: Where did you grow up? Do you have siblings? Did you always want to be in your current field? What's your vision for your next year? What's your favorite place to travel? What are your hobbies? What's your favorite part of your day? Everyone has something in their story you can learn from, if you just take the time to listen.

When you focus on building deep, lifelong relationships, you will directly impact your long-term happiness and fulfillment.

It may be tempting to only expand your network by meeting with people who work in your field, but it's important to cast a wider net. Cultivating relationships within your industry will feel comfortable, but remember that growth requires discomfort! There is a power in meeting people with whom you have nothing in common. Some of them will open your mind to ideas you never would've considered on your own or from just chatting among your own colleagues. I've met rocket scientists and chefs who have taught me more about business and entrepreneurship than some of the seasoned executives I've spent time with.

One of the simplest and most effective ways to expand your network is also the cheapest. If you've got four dollars for a cup of coffee, you've got an excuse to meet with someone new and begin a relationship.

Why am I championing something as simple as coffee dates? Because they've changed my own life for the better. A few years ago, I spent four dollars on a cup of coffee with someone who ended up being one of the most important mentors of my life. This experience had such a profound effect on me that I purposely block off time in my calendar every week to either connect with people already in my network or meet with someone new. Many of the seemingly random coffee meetings I've attended have introduced me to people and ideas that changed my life in unexpected and wonderful ways.

Coffee can lead to a new job, a promotion, a partnership, an investment, a new client, a mentorship, or even a lifelong friendship. Building connections can spark new ideas, help you make key decisions, and help you see outcomes, roadblocks, and opportunities you may not have otherwise been aware of. Discussions over coffee create momentum and can put you one step closer to what you've been working toward and striving for. Here is a simple template you can use to reach out to your first few coffee dates. Feel free to build on it and customize, but also remember that simple and to-the-point always works well!

Dear [name],

I really admire what you have achieved in [____] and would love to connect with you for coffee and learn more about your path to success. My own goal is to [____], so I would particularly like to speak with you about your experience with [____]. I understand you are extremely busy, and I can make myself available to suit your schedule. Please let me know what works best.

I'm excited to connect,

[Your name]

Now a word of warning: Do *not* be transactional when you meet with a new connection. Don't reach out to someone simply to get something immediate in return. If you do get something from your very first meeting with a new connection, that's great . . . but understand there are no guarantees. Don't focus as much on what you can get as what you can learn. One of the most important things you can do to show your gratitude is to come to the meeting prepared. Research your questions. Write down what you want to ask; that way, if you get overwhelmed or excited, you won't forget which topics you want to cover. Show up, be on time, and be present for every moment of the time you spend together. And don't forget to send a thoughtful thank-you note afterward!

Building and expanding your network is an ongoing process. It's something you'll do for the rest of your life, and your network will only grow if you invest your time and attention into it. So make genuine connections, and then take good care of them. I promise they'll take good care of you in return.

BUILD BRIDGES; DON'T BURN THEM

I truly love connecting with people in my own life . . . and one of my superpowers is connecting the people I meet to *other* people I think they should know. I'm always trying to amplify the reach of my network and help others build theirs. One of my goals when I meet someone new is to introduce them to someone else who can support them. I rifle through my mental contact list to find anyone who can help them on their journey to success, and I make a point of facilitating an introduction. I find it so fulfilling to be the conduit, the one who says, "Ah! I know just the right person for that!"

I've been this way since I had braces. Even when I was a preteen I was trying to set up my friends with dates to the middle school dance. If a schoolmate said they wanted to earn some extra cash, I'd introduce them to my boss at the pizza parlor or neighborhood parents who needed babysitters. My grandma always told me it's better to include than exclude, and I took her word for it, busily making connections throughout the years and throughout my life. Granted, this got me in trouble sometimes, like when I invited *all* of my ex-boyfriends to my pool party. But I've always wanted to err on the side of overincluding because I believe that opening up my social circle will help everyone I know help expand theirs.

I hope that you'll follow my lead in your network-building efforts. To make the most of the time and energy you'll expend, I strongly recommend becoming a connector of people yourself—and taking my grandma's advice about being inclusive in big, broad, generous ways!

Not everyone adopts this approach, of course. Some people seem protective of their relationships and don't want to share them with others. That's not my perspective. In fact, I believe that safeguarding your connections will hurt you in the long run. By maintaining a closed, insular network, you're limiting the opportunities that could enrich your life. You're adopting a mindset of scarcity. I've never felt that way. Especially when it comes to relationships and connections, I've found that the more you share, the more you create. So, as you build your own network, try to be generous with your connections. Next time a friend tells you about a goal she's trying to achieve, ask yourself, *Do I know anyone who could help her?* If you do, make an introduction. Next time you meet someone with knowledge or experience that could benefit a colleague, connect those two people. It never hurts to pay it forward.

My beliefs about the importance of sharing and nurturing connections come from a lifetime of working to build bridges instead of burning them. As a natural connector myself, I've always done my best to create and maintain relationships even if things get a bit rocky. The world is a small place, and you never know when you might need to work with someone again.

I've worked with thousands of people over two decades, and my biggest takeaway for anyone who is leaving a company is this: exit as gracefully as you entered. The way you leave will become inextricable from your reputation. Even if you get fired, you can still move on respectfully and without burning bridges! I think of it this way: you should put in as much work to make a good impression when you leave a job as you do when you try to get a job, because your reputation follows you and you have to think of behaving in ways that help your personal brand. A word to the wise: if you're planning on leaving a company, make sure you speak to your manager before you speak to your coworkers.

I can remember one young employee who worked for me right out of college. She was a real superstar with an excellent work ethic, so she was promoted quickly. Because of this, it was a bit of a slap in the face when she left work one day to work at one of our competitor companies. Not only did she leave disrespectfully without giving us sufficient notice, but she actively tried to hire my current employees to join her by disparaging our company. I promise that scorching the earth when you leave is one of the least pragmatic and intelligent things you can do for your career and reputation. She left by burning a bridge, and in doing so she lost the opportunity for sustained support and advocacy from me for the rest of her career.

On the flip side, I've had hundreds of experiences that remind me of the value and power of preserving and protecting the bridges. A story I often think about is how one of my senior executives (and close friends) acted when the company we were building together underwent a cultural shift. What was once a fast-paced, flexible entrepreneurial environment had turned into one that was more structured and corporate. This culture change did *not* fit many employees who'd been working for me for years, especially this executive. He and I had a difference in opinion about the direction in which I was steering the company. He was a very talented and skilled individual, but we constantly disagreed, and it was exhausting to both of us. We eventually came to a mutual decision that, out of respect for each other and our relationship, it would be best if he left so we didn't incur permanent damage. Doing this actually enabled him to work in an entrepreneurial, startup-style environment, which is exactly the situation he thrives in. He was a perfect example of someone who made an Opportunity Jump and left but actively worked on strengthening our existing bridge. We remain close to this day. In fact, I invested in the company he started and joined the board!

This experience underlines my belief that leaving doesn't have to be the end of a relationship. When it's done thoughtfully and respectfully, it can be the start to an even better one.

THE POWER OF GIVING

I believe there's nothing more powerful than giving without expecting to get anything in return. To successfully forge deep, long-lasting connections, you need to offer your help, time, and resources with no expectation of reciprocation. Giving comes from your heart.

One of my favorite movies is *Pay It Forward*. It tells the story of a social studies teacher who gives an audacious assignment to his junior high school class: come up with an idea that will change the world for the better and then put it into action. When one student creates a plan for "paying forward" favors he receives, he not only improves the life of his struggling single mom but also sets in motion an unprecedented wave of human kindness. This simple and beautiful story proves that each person can make a difference in the world by doing good, and that positive actions can have a domino effect. Even small acts of generosity and empathy can have a huge impact. *Pay It Forward* also reveals that we'll probably never see or understand how deeply our acts of compassion affect others. Giving is far more powerful when it is done with no strings attached.

This applies to the attitude you should have while building your network too. If you approach relationships with a short-term, self-focused attitude, it will eventually backfire on you; I guarantee it. If you set out to make connections only with the mindset of "What can I get?" instead of "What can I give?" the connections you make will likely be superficial and fleeting. Yes, it takes more energy and effort to help others while also helping yourself, but the payoff is worth the investment. The jump you're planning may only take six months or a year to complete, but it will affect the trajectory of your entire life. So will the network you create to support that jump. This is a long-term strategy, not a quick fix. Relationships should never be temporary or disposable. They should be enduring and supportive and treated with great care. They should be shared and paid forward, even when it feels inconvenient to do so.

Keep that in mind as you reach out to people. Be grateful for the help you're given while always thinking about the help you can give to others. Approach network building with a mindset of abundance, and give fully without expecting anything in return.

MAKE PEOPLE A PRIORITY

I'm passionate about nurturing and investing in my relationships . . . but I'm also not perfect. Like everyone, I drop the ball now and then. A few years ago, I was so distracted by a deal I was trying to close that I didn't pick up on one of my trusted employees' cries for help. She dropped hints that she was experiencing stress and conflict with her boss, but since they'd always had a difficult relationship, I overlooked it as an immediate problem and figured it would work itself out eventually. I listened when she called me, but I didn't hear the subtext. Because I was traveling so much, I didn't have the chance to meet with her in person, so the subtle cues she was giving me were lost in translation over the phone. So, when she dropped her letter of resignation on my desk, I was blindsided. And I was deeply, *deeply* disappointed in myself for not reading between the lines. That experience taught me an important lesson. It reinforced the power and importance of active listening in my life. Active listening requires you to be fully present and hear what is being said—and what's not being said—so you can really understand the whole picture. I pay attention to someone's body language, the words they're choosing, if they look me in the eye. These subtle cues are indicators of bigger issues under the surface.

The experience with my trusted employee taught me to proactively check in with the important people in my life. Just by making myself available as a sympathetic ear or sounding board, I was able to support many more people through unexpected hardships. By making my people a priority, I deepened my relationships even further.

Life isn't all about work or money or even success. In the end, relationships are truly what matters most. As you progress through your one-year success plan and your life starts to get busier, make sure you're devoting enough time to the relationships that are most important in your life. Be intentional about who you spend your time with; you only have twenty-four hours in a day, so make each moment count! And show your gratitude to the people who support you by supporting *them* in return. When you recognize and celebrate the strengths of others, you uplift people and strengthen your bonds.

And those strong bonds mean you'll always have the support, enthusiasm, and expertise of an amazing group of people. Who could ask for a better measure of success than that?

Chapter 7 Jump Prep

- Find a mentor! Do you have a mentor in your life who can support and advise you when you jump? If not, take the steps to find one. First, brainstorm a few great mentors and think about whether they would be good matches for you. Then reach out on LinkedIn, send an email, or make a phone call.

- Think about the last time you went out of your way to give something to someone else (your time, a connection, a referral, advice, etc.) without expecting anything in return. If it's been a while, make an effort to do at least three things to pay it forward and build relationships this month.

- Next time you meet someone new, ask thoughtful questions and spend 80 percent of the time actively listening.

Chapter 7 Jump Hacks

- Too many people believe that asking for help is the equivalent of asking for a favor. Unless you want tons of someone's time or are asking someone to divulge top secret insider info, they'll probably be delighted to help you! So here's your hack: Ask. Ask for advice, insights, and opinions from people you admire and trust. If they don't have the answers, ask them, "Do you know someone else who could help me with this?"

- Get in the habit of both asking for and *giving* help! Find two people you can help, and find two people who can help you. Networking must go both ways!

- Three of the most powerful words you can say in your life are "Let's have coffee." Commit to one coffee date per month as part of your one-year success plan, and make at least one of them with someone who could help you make or support your jump.

CHAPTER

8

TAP INTO YOUR INNER
STRENGTH

Strength is not always physical; it is also mental and emotional. Even when fear and doubt say we can't, we can. We have the courage and ability to keep going, put one foot in front of the other, and continue working toward our goals. I often feel an overwhelming rush of challenging, intimidating emotions when I make jumps of my own, but I try my hardest not to let them stop me. Perseverance is strength. Facing tough circumstances and not giving up is strength. You have a well of inner strength—we all do—and it's time to tap into it.

Someone who embodies courage, perseverance, and confidence is US senator Tammy Duckworth. Long before she was elected to office, she was deployed to Iraq as a Black Hawk helicopter pilot for the National Guard in 2004. In November of that same year, her helicopter was hit by a rocket-propelled grenade. Tammy was so horrifically injured by the crash that her copilot assumed she was dead.[1]

Tammy lost both of her legs to amputation and nearly lost her right arm, which was saved after a grueling thirteen-hour-long emergency surgery. But her inner strength and will to live were unshakable. Against all odds, Tammy survived.

She spent an entire year recovering at Walter Reed National Military Medical Center, where she quickly became an advocate for her fellow soldiers.[2] After a life change this devastating and drastic, many people would (understandably) want to remove themselves from public life, but not Tammy! She continued to persevere. And in 2012, Tammy was elected to Congress. That's right; she was so determined to fight for veterans' rights that she ran for public office. When talking about her decision to enter politics, Tammy said, "My experience in Iraq made me realize, and during the recovery, that I could have died. And I just had to do more with my life." Instead of letting an incredibly devastating experience leave her living a life of hopelessness and pain, she used it as fuel to propel her forward. With this story in mind, you might ask yourself, "How can I use my current experiences as fuel to propel myself forward?"

After just four years of working as a congresswoman, Tammy was elected as a US senator, becoming the first disabled woman and the second Asian American woman in the Senate. *And!* In April 2018, Tammy became the first senator to give birth while holding office.[3] She broke multiple glass ceilings and continues to forge her path in the face of challenges. She uses her fiery passion to advocate for gender equality and environmental justice and to support US veterans. She is an intellectually and emotionally strong powerhouse who has continually faced outspoken criticism of her views without backing down. I admire her so much for the consistent courage she's shown throughout her entire career.

Tammy is an inspiring example of a courageous person who was able to channel her inner strength to persevere and overcome the odds. I believe everyone can take inspiration from Tammy's story, even if their goals and challenges are quite different from hers. She shows us all that strength is an inner resource, and a renewable one at that. We are all stronger than we think.

The truth is, you're going to face considerable uncertainty between the time you jump and the time you land. With that in mind, let's look at some ways to cultivate and strengthen the courage, perseverance, and confidence you already have inside you.

BUILDING EMOTIONAL COURAGE

Before we get into the specifics of emotional courage, let me make one thing clear: courage is not the absence of fear. Courageous people feel fear, too, but they are able to manage and overcome that fear so it does not stop them from taking action. All people feel fear, and fear is a valuable emotion. We don't need to eradicate it; we just need to learn how to work with it and use it in productive ways.

That's where emotional courage becomes one of the most useful tools in your emotional tool kit. Leading vulnerability researcher Brené Brown describes the attribute as "having the courage to show up when you can't control the outcome."[4] In her book *Daring Greatly*, Brown insists that emotional courage and vulnerability are crucial to helping us lead, love, work, and parent more effectively. She encourages us to bravely feel the full spectrum of both negative and positive emotions as a means of inoculating ourselves against fear.

For example, imagine that you need to have a difficult conversation with a coworker, friend, or family member . . . but you've been avoiding the conversation. You're afraid you're going to make them angry, you're afraid you're going to hurt their feelings, or you're afraid that the discussion will turn into a big fight. So, instead of facing the issue head-on, you make excuses about why now is not the right time. This is where emotional courage comes in. it gives you the confidence to feel more comfortable addressing your fears instead of ignoring them. Emotional courage is a common trait among many of the most successful people I've worked with. They've trained themselves to be able to feel uncomfortable feelings and have hard conversations, because successful people know that not addressing the hard thing head-on will hurt more in the long run.

Truthfully, this is something I struggle with every day. Building the courage to confront people is something I consciously have to work on. So trust me, I understand how hard this can be and that changing it will not happen overnight. I recommend starting small to build your muscle for emotional courage. Here are a few exercises that will help you hone your ability to embrace your feelings and build emotional bravery:

- Speak up in a meeting when you normally would not.

- Have a hard conversation with a friend or family member.

- Give constructive feedback to a coworker.

- Admit your fears and show vulnerability.

- Practice being direct in low-risk situations.

Emotional courage is a muscle, and like all muscles it gets stronger the more you exercise it. Each time you have a hard conversation, admit your fears, and show vulnerability, you are building your emotional courage.

Facebook COO Sheryl Sandberg was forced to dig deep into her reserves of emotional courage when her husband died suddenly at the age of forty-seven. A natural-born problem-solver, she found herself faced with a problem that had no solution: grief. Sheryl took some time to process her loss on her own. Eventually, she chose to talk publicly about one of her life's most painful experiences in hopes of helping others. She wrote *Option B: Facing Adversity, Building Resilience, and Finding Joy*. Although she made sure the book was packed with advice to help people push on and bounce back from horrible misfortune, she didn't shy away from sharing her feelings about loss. She shared the raw, painful emotions she felt after her husband died, showing tremendous emotional courage. Instead of bottling them up, she allowed herself to feel those awful feelings and share them with her readers. She chose to be vulnerable publicly in hopes that doing so would help change the conversation around adversity.

Sheryl also made the choice to talk with people about the resilience and growth that follows a painful loss, a topic that is often seen as taboo. By publicly sharing her journey through grief, Sheryl normalized the conversation on a topic that people would usually rather sweep under the rug. She and her coauthor, psychologist Adam Grant, frame post-traumatic growth as the ways in which we grow in our lives after death, loss, and failure.

"Post-traumatic growth doesn't mean that it's overall more positive," she explains. "I would trade all the growth to have Dave back. But I'm closer with my parents than I was. I'm closer with my closest friends than I was. I have more appreciation. I have more perspective."[5]

Like Sheryl, we can all choose to be more emotionally courageous in the face of hardship. We can feel our discomfort without letting it defeat us. Practicing this and building the muscle for your jump will help you be more resilient once you land and beyond. Here are some simple ways to amplify your emotional courage:

- *Build Confidence by Recognizing Confidence:* I've noticed that in order to develop confidence in yourself, you've got to *start* with some confidence—like a seed that needs planting and nurturing. Luckily, no matter how unsure you may feel overall, there are some areas where you already have confidence. So your first step is to recognize where you already feel independent and strong. Who helps you feel energized and empowered? In what situations do you feel grounded? Noticing this will help you feel it more deeply and allow you to build on it. For example, if you identify as an introvert and feel courageous when you're supporting a charismatic leader as second-in-command, you can put yourself in situations where you're in partnership with others.

- *Resist Temptation:* This might not sound like fun, but it sure does fortify your emotional courage! Practice feeling and resisting temptation. Go into your favorite boutique and don't buy anything, or stroll through your local bakery and only buy a cup of coffee. What's the point of this self-inflicted torture? When temptation doesn't break your commitments, then you've flexed your emotional-courage muscle.

- *Notice, Observe, and Embrace Your Feelings:* Since emotional courage is all about feeling the full spectrum of both negative and positive emotions, you've got to train yourself to recognize and get comfortable with them all. When a strong feeling hits you, start by noticing it and naming it. Then make some observations about how it's affecting you. What is it doing within your body? If you're feeling nervous, where does that feeling reside? Your stomach? Your shoulders? Once you've noticed and observed, do your best to accept the feeling instead of fighting it. Accept that you're having a strong emotion, and allow it to work its way through you. Remember that most emotions only last ninety seconds, so once you've gone through this process, you'll be amazed by how quickly feelings will dissipate.

OVERCOMING SELF-DOUBT

We all doubt ourselves sometimes. Doubt can feel like a self-made prison that keeps you locked inside your own insecurities. It's usually the negative soundtrack of your inner voices telling you not to take action. But more often than not, it's a mirage of negativity—you just have to be able to see through it! And trust me, I know how hard that is; I've also dealt with the cynical effects of trusting my doubt more than my true ability. Early on in my career, I passed up many opportunities I was actually perfect for because the voices of self-doubt in my head convinced me I wasn't qualified! These are the types of thoughts that held me back:

- You're definitely going to fail.

- You don't have enough experience.

- People are going to notice that you don't meet the qualifications.

I felt all of these doubts when I was asked to join my first corporate board. At first, I was ecstatic! It was an honor, and it felt like such a milestone in my career, I had to say yes . . . right? But then the voice of doubt started to creep in:

- I've never been on a board before.

- All the other board members have fancy degrees and MBAs.

- What if they find out I'm not qualified?

The other board members were all men, were twenty years older than me, and had spent their entire careers as investors. I was an operator with no investment experience at the time. I was nothing like the other people on the board, so how could I possibly be a good fit? My feelings of self-doubt and unworthiness spiraled, and I ended up making an excuse about why I couldn't join the board.

Five years later, I was at a dinner with one of the board members, and he asked me why I'd declined the offer. I told him I didn't believe I had enough experience as an investor. He said, "We wanted you to join *because* of your digital expertise and your operating experience running a company." He told me that they were pursuing me to join because they wanted a well-rounded board with a diversity of experience. I was shocked and disappointed that I had just assumed I wasn't qualified, when in reality the experience I had made me the ideal board member. My self-doubt stopped me from taking on an amazing career opportunity. So, from that moment on, I made a commitment to myself to push past my insecurities and trust myself and my abilities. I was determined not to let that happen again. I decided that whenever a new and exciting project or opportunity showed up in my life, instead of saying no when my insecurities, doubts, or fears reared their ugly heads, I would say yes, even if I didn't feel fully qualified or ready.

I said yes to: new projects, new partnerships, new clients, new countries, and new boards. I pushed myself to give terrifying presentations, I cold-called investors asking for money, and I embraced negotiating business deals with people I thought would say no. I turned saying yes and moving beyond my self-doubt into a practice.

It's totally human and normal to doubt ourselves. Women especially fall prey to this tendency. Did you know that most men will apply for a job when they meet only 60 percent of the qualifications, but many women will apply only if they meet 100 percent of them?[6] Even though studies have consistently shown that companies employing women in large numbers perform better, women individually struggle with self-doubt—so much so that social scientists have named the phenomenon the confidence gap.[7] Women also tend to struggle with impostor syndrome more than men. Even famous and wildly successful women have reported that they worry constantly they don't deserve the praise they receive.

Self-doubt is poison. It plagues many of us and holds us back from chasing our dreams. Luckily, it can be managed—and even defeated—with the right tools and mindset.

Here are three strategies I use for dealing with self-doubt.

1. *Make a List of Your Top Accomplishments:* Think of this like a highlight reel of your successes in life. It will serve as a reminder of past wins and give you confidence that you will succeed again if you put in the hard work.

2. *Reframe Inexperience:* When you are doing something new, remind yourself that you are a beginner, not an imposter. It takes time to become an expert, and every expert started as a beginner.

3. *Give Yourself Advice:* Ask yourself what you would say to a friend with the same destructive thought patterns. I'm sure you wouldn't be as negative or defeatist with them as you are with yourself. Help yourself realize how far-fetched and unfounded your doubts are.

Making changes in your personal or professional life is hard enough without your inner voice telling you that you are unqualified or unprepared. Having strategies to overcome self-doubt will make it easier to take your jump. When you learn to conquer those feelings of inadequacy and focus on the positive, you are training your subconscious to be your ally and not your enemy. You will be equipped and ready to choose hope, confidence, and optimism even when the road ahead looks impossible.

OPTIMISM IS A CHOICE

Optimism is not just blind happiness; it's a conscious decision to live your life with a positive attitude. Optimists like me believe that good things will happen regardless of the setbacks along the way. And trust me, I've had my fair share of setbacks:

I've been laid off.

I've been broke.

I've been bankrupt.

I've been criticized.

I've been rejected.

I've been mocked.

I've been doubted.

I've lost my biggest clients.

I've lost my best employees.

I've lost business partners.

I've been served.

I've been sued.

I've had times when I was terrified, exhausted, and wanted to give up.

… But I didn't.

When setbacks come into the path of your jump (and they will), it can be tempting to focus solely on the negative. You may feel the urge to only see what's right in front of you instead of expanding your view to consider any potential positive long-term outcomes. Make sure you never allow setbacks to deplete one of your most important resources: your optimism. In times of crisis, it's more important than ever to zero in on the good.

The creators of some of your favorite animated films are intimately familiar with the power of choosing to be optimistic rather than pessimistic. In 1994, animated film studio Pixar was in trouble. The company was hemorrhaging money because the movie it was about to release, *Toy Story*, had gone way over budget. Six million dollars over budget, to be exact. Microsoft had expressed interest in buying Pixar—primarily to acquire its 3D graphic-design software—but the deal was called off at the last minute. Things were looking pretty grim for Pixar in advance of *Toy Story*'s release.

That didn't deter Pixar's internal creative and leadership teams, though. As they were putting the finishing touches on *Toy Story* and wondering what the future might hold for Pixar, several top creatives met for lunch to discuss possible new projects. Over that one fateful lunch, they brainstormed story outlines for *A Bug's Life*, *Monsters, Inc.*, and *WALL-E*, all of which became blockbuster hits. Instead of focusing on the possible collapse of their company, they assumed they'd pull through and poured their energy into envisioning new creative work. In a time of financial uncertainty, they chose optimism. If they'd spent that lunch meeting making plans to sell off their servers and make massive layoffs, those brilliant movies might never have been made![8]

Pessimism is a self-fulfilling prophecy. If you believe the worst will happen, you are paving the way for it to come crashing into your life. Fortunately, optimism works similarly. By maintaining a positive attitude and searching for the good hidden within challenging situations, you make space for good things to unfold.

In order to make a successful jump, it helps to train your brain to be more optimistic, to consistently look at the bright side of things. Here are a few strategies I use in my own life:

Practice Positive Self-Talk

Your inner voice is talking to you all day. To help your subconscious create a positivity loop, write out a few positive affirmations and put them where you will see them. I have a pinboard of positive messages in my bathroom that I read each morning while I get ready and before I go to bed at night. It sets the tone for the day and my dreams. Here are a few examples:

- I have the power to make my dreams come true.

- I am excited about the next stage of my career.

- I am proud of myself and all that I have, and *will*, accomplish.

- Today is going to be a great day!

Curate the Media You Consume

We are what we eat, and the media we consume is not so different from the food we put in our bodies. Our digital diet influences how we learn, what we think, and how we feel. So be conscious of what you're reading, listening to, watching, and following on social media. Because the content you feed your brain affects your subconscious.

Focus on What You Can Control

Worrying about things outside of your control is a waste of time and depletes your positivity. The past is the past, and you're not going that way anyway. Focus on the future and what you can do today, and fuel your journey with the optimism it deserves.

Stop Complaining

I always tell my kids (and myself) that if they don't have anything nice to say, they shouldn't say anything at all. This is the same for complaining. Complaining is a vicious cycle, and it spurs more complaining! Challenge yourself to stop complaining for twenty-four hours. Every time you have the urge to complain, say something positive instead. You will be amazed by how this improves your mood, your attitude, and your mindset.

Be Grateful

At the end of every day, reflect on the good things that happened and what you are grateful for. My husband and I do this with our kids at dinner every night to reinforce the positives and teach them to be grateful for even the small gifts. We basically rehearse for Thanksgiving 364 days a year.

Choosing to remain optimistic can be tough at times, especially if you're preparing for a Survival Jump to escape a tough situation. It's crucial to remember, though, that optimism *is* a choice. How you view and react to the world around you is within your control. When it comes to tapping your inner strength, choosing optimism is one of the simplest (and most magical) strategies you can employ to keep your mind focused and your spirits high.

JUMPING INTO THE UNKNOWN

Most of us aren't especially eager to admit our fear to ourselves . . . or anyone else, for that matter. Instead, we find ways to stall or delay. Maybe in your case, you come up with a long list of excuses for why you can't take that life-changing leap and head out on your own. You might snuggle up in your comfort zone, insisting that you'd rather keep working your steady job than embrace your creative side and start a side hustle.

I know better. And you can too. Once you recognize the signs and acknowledge that fear is the main thing that's holding you back, you can finally start to conquer your fears and take control of your life—no matter how uncertain the future may feel right now. Although there will be uncertainty between the time you jump and the time you land, don't let that deter you. There will be challenges, roadblocks, and setbacks, but *hang on*! Have courage! And tap into your inner strength whenever you need it. You can do this!

Chapter 8 Jump Prep

- Which of these strategies have you used to build your own emotional courage? The best way to identify what will work for you in the future is to look at what's worked for you in the past. Make a note of which of these tactics you know work for you—and which ones you'd like to try next.

- Identify situations and circumstances where you are most likely to experience self-doubt. Is it moving into the new and unknown? Perhaps it's when others are watching and you're worried about what they are thinking? Maybe it's when you feel you don't have enough experience or expertise in something? Or when you don't have a plan? Know your self-doubt triggers, and commit to using the techniques from this chapter to combat them!

- Look for the positive in challenging situations. Next time you encounter a setback, use it as an opportunity to try one of these techniques and tap into your inner strength. The more you flex this muscle, the stronger it will become.

Chapter 8 Jump Hacks

- Write out a few positive affirmations and put them where you will see them. When you see them consistently, and you believe them, you will see positive change.

- The quickest way to reduce your comparative tendencies is to take a break from social media. People post their most exciting and glamorous moments *only*, but our brains forget that and we assume we're seeing the entirety of their lives. Someone once said, "Don't compare your feature film to someone else's highlight reel," and that's exactly what social media is! Step away when you're feeling overwhelmed. Remind yourself that you're only seeing the highlights.

CHAPTER

9

STOP CARING
WHAT OTHER PEOPLE THINK

I've never been someone who fits in very easily. I've always pushed the limits, taken risks, and gone after whatever I wanted. Forget the black and white; I live in the bright pink. (I hate gray.) When I was younger, early in my career, I tried to dial back my energy so I could be more like my peers. But dialing back my energy was a mistake; it made me miserable. Why spend time making yourself more acceptable for someone else? You may lose a part of your greatness in the process.

Standing out is lonely. It's awkward. It's scary.

But you have to be different to make a difference.

I know all this now, but when I was in grade school, I definitely worried about fitting in. I wanted to be accepted and liked, even though trying to be like everyone else made me deeply unhappy. I wasn't like everybody else. Instead of playing with dolls and having tea parties, I wanted to ride a unicycle and walk on stilts. Instead of playing team sports, I wanted to ride horses and downhill ski. As it turned out, the things that held me back from fitting in—my willingness to be different, work hard, and take risks; my relentless optimism; and my refusal to take no for an answer—became the very things that fueled my success. I learned early on that strict rules and norms aren't great for creativity. Neither is judgment, embarrassment, or shame. So I gave myself the space to be who I was instead of trying to be what everyone expected me to be.

And since the jump you are planning is likely to ruffle some feathers and draw some criticism, I want to prepare you to do the same. Give yourself permission to turn down the volume on your critics, trust your vision, and learn the difference between constructive advice and unhelpful nitpicking.

This whole chapter has just one goal: to prove that *your own opinion of yourself* is much more important than the opinions of other people.

PEOPLE-PLEASING IS A LOSING BATTLE

Okay, quick reality check: it is perfectly normal to care what certain people think of you. Especially your inner circle, family, spouse or partner, close friends, boss, and those who have your best interests at heart.

However! There's a fine line between respecting the opinions and beliefs of others and bending over backward to please them. Especially when the trade-off is your own success.

One of the start-up founders I invested in had this wake-up call when she had to decide between prioritizing her own success or continuing to struggle behind the scenes to "look good" for everyone else:

After five years, countless investors, and millions of dollars raised, I woke up one morning and realized I just couldn't do it anymore. As any entrepreneur must be, I am incredibly resilient. I kept telling myself I would find a solution to get us back on track.

Months went by with no success, and I started to wonder why I couldn't admit what was staring me directly in the face: my business had failed. But how could I possibly call my investors and let them know they were going to lose their money? Or tell my employees that had been with me from the beginning that they no longer had a job and their equity was worthless? I was so worried about what other people would think that I wasn't being honest with myself.

It's important to know in life when to cut your losses and start fresh. I knew I had given it everything I had, and that's all people could ask of me. It wasn't easy, but I made those hard phone calls to my investors, told my employees and my family. And guess what? At the end of the day, I survived.

If there's one thing I've learned from this experience, it's that pretending everything was okay hurt me the most. Trying to keep everyone happy was impossible, and I was just prolonging the inevitable.

Think about your mindsets and behaviors for a moment. Do you go out of your way to make others feel comfortable, even if it means sacrificing your own valuable time or resources? Do you say yes when you want desperately to say no? Do you feel consumed by worry if you know you've upset someone in your life, even over something small or insignificant? If so, you may be a people-pleaser. I'm totally one. I'm also living proof that knowing is half the battle:

---

after I recognized this about myself, I was able to control my impulses and put my own needs first.

If you're like me and have this personality type, you may value the needs and viewpoints of others so highly that they essentially eclipse your own. And even if you aren't a people-pleaser at all times, you may engage in people-pleasing behaviors, especially when you're making big changes in your life. This instinct is one that scientists believe is hardwired into our brains, which means it can be tough to fight. Studies have shown that we all have a fundamental need to belong, to be accepted and liked by those around us. Saying no, pushing back, and even standing up for ourselves can cause friction. We all know this instinctively and may avoid those behaviors to feed our need to gain approval from people in our lives. It's so much easier to just say yes or be quiet or take the path of least resistance.

Easier, but not always better.

A people-pleaser friend of mine works as a human resources consultant, which is an especially tough line of work for anyone with this personality type. Since she's an outside advisor who swoops in to solve business problems, her number one job is to help identify solutions to her clients' problems and make their lives easier. My friend was constantly bidding on contracts, landing work, and being asked to do more than was in the agreed-upon scope of work. And because there was no such thing as "out of scope" in her world, she often did the extra work without speaking up. She created a cycle that was nearly impossible to break. She built a great reputation of going above and beyond that eventually proved self-defeating. It meant that her clients assumed she would do extra work without additional compensation. By prioritizing their needs over hers, she made herself miserable and, ultimately, bitter.

That's one of the dangers of being a people-pleaser. Your own well-meaning actions can backfire. When my friend told me what was going on, I encouraged her to change her contract so that she got paid an hourly rate for anything outside the scope of work. This change put her back in the driver's seat and made her feel valued and respected.

Caring what certain people think of you is fine, but caring too much can get really destructive. Constantly saying yes to others will force you to spend less time on yourself and less energy focusing on things that really matter to you. When you prioritize the happiness and comfort of others but fail to do the same for yourself, resentments may start to build. What starts as a desire to please others can mutate into a truly unhealthy behavior pattern if you don't learn to control the urge and redirect the energy into yourself.

People-pleasing can even negatively impact your sense of self. When you only care about how other people feel, you can get caught up in guessing how they want you to be. You might start to change your behaviors or sugarcoat your opinions to get them to like you.

See how this can be a slippery slope?

I've slid down that slope several times myself. At my first job, I had an extremely demanding boss. He was smart and savvy and had the ability to make me feel like I was on top of the world when the work I did impressed him. So, as a people-pleaser, I ran myself ragged trying to earn his approval. I worked insane hours, surpassed every sales goal he set, and drove my team hard and relentlessly in hopes of pleasing him. Sometimes it worked; sometimes it didn't. And since

I'm always looking for patterns in the world around me, I noticed that the pattern with this boss was that . . . there was no pattern. There was no rhyme or reason to his behavior. If I crushed a sales goal and told him on Tuesday, he might celebrate my win, but if I waited until Thursday, he might ignore or dismiss my good news.

Once I noticed this inconsistency, I couldn't unsee it. This boss was reacting to me based on his moods, not my performance. My experience with him taught me that the only thing that would genuinely make me happy was to do the best job I could and not allow my happiness to hinge solely on his response.

Once you start living your life *for yourself* instead of for other people, amazing things happen. Invest your energy into becoming the best possible version of yourself instead of trying to gain everyone else's approval. Your differences are your strengths and are what make you powerful.

ACCENTUATE THE POSITIVE; ELIMINATE THE NEGATIVE

Some of you might be saying, "Easier said than done, Kim. I'm already anxious about my jump. How am I supposed to focus on the positive if the people I trust are giving negative feedback about the choices I'm making?"

I hear you on this issue.

It is extremely hard to trust yourself when others express mistrust. It's a struggle to move past criticism and take negative comments in stride . . . partially because of that ingrained negativity bias. We naturally tend to cling to negative comments while forgetting positive ones.[1] Just one nasty joke or sarcastic comment can send us into a downward spiral. This tendency has been ingrained into human evolution, and for good reason: it kept us out of harm's way. When we were hunter-gatherers, our skill at dodging danger was what kept us alive! So our brains developed systems that made it possible for us to notice and remember danger, fear, and negativity.[2]

That was great for prehistoric people, but it's not so great for those of us living in the present.

To take your jump in the face of pushback, you will need to be aware of the negativity bias, so you can reduce its impact on your success. Here are three practices that will help you resist the downward drag of negative input, advice, and opinions.

Keep a Gratitude Journal

There's endless research proving that gratitude is beneficial and that practicing it helps us with everything from anxiety and depression to building healthy relationships.[3] One of the things I do to make sure I appreciate the good things in my life is keep a gratitude journal. It's a near-daily diary of things that make me feel grateful that helps me focus my attention squarely on the positive. I highly recommend this for anyone who struggles with negativity, people-pleasing, or self-doubt. It will help you remember everything you love and value when you're facing negativity about your jump. (Or anything else in your life!)

Savor the Moment

Like many of you, I lead a very busy life, and it's easy to get distracted or overwhelmed. So I've learned to make a conscious effort to recognize enjoyable experiences as they're taking place. When you pause to "drink in" a positive moment, you're savoring it and creating memories. Think of it like creating a memory bank of positive experiences. Doing this helps you retrain your brain and build resistance to negativity and doubt. Creating a stockpile of positive mental images and emotions can help you address the imbalance that negativity bias creates.

Mindfulness Exercise

Dr. Russ Harris specializes in acceptance and commitment therapy (ACT), which uses mindfulness strategies to increase psychological flexibility. One of the core practices of ACT is diffusing your thoughts, which Dr. Harris describes as "the ability to separate from your thoughts and let them come and go, instead of getting caught up in them or allowing them to dictate what you do."[4] I've found diffusion extremely helpful in dealing with painful, unhelpful, or self-defeating thoughts and beliefs. One diffusion technique I love asks you to add the phrase "I notice I am having the thought . . ." to negative or judgmental thoughts. As in, "I notice I am having the thought that taking this jump is a huge mistake." Doing this helps you view your thoughts as thoughts, rather than fundamental truths or realities. Reframing thoughts—especially ones that stem from negative input from other people—puts some distance between you and those thoughts.

Our brains may be wired to hyperfocus on the negative instead of the positive, but we can rewire them. With these techniques, you will eventually develop a healthy immunity to criticism and naysaying. And doing this will be especially helpful to people-pleasers who dread critiques and commentary from the people in their lives. Fighting negativity bias will help you hear the fears and doubts of other people and jump anyway. It will help you care less about what others say and think about your plans, your dreams, your vision for the future. This is so important. If you want to make a difference in the world—or even if you just want to make a massive change in your own life—I guarantee you will encounter opposition.

And as long as you're prepared to face that opposition and trust yourself despite it, nothing can stop you.

THE ONLY OPINION THAT
MATTERS IS YOURS

Everybody has an opinion—especially about what society deems as normal or not normal, what is good or bad, and what they think is right or wrong. But out of the trillions of opinions, the only opinion that really counts is your own—though I know firsthand how hard it is not to care what people think.

Having children was a gift I had been waiting for my whole life. I had always assumed I'd have a giant family, since I came from one: my father's parents were married over sixty years and had five boys, sixteen grandkids, and twenty-eight great-grandkids. But starting the family of my dreams proved to be more difficult for me than most. I failed to get pregnant and spent close to a decade trying everything, including numerous in vitro fertilization (IVF), with no success. Out of options, my husband and I decided to try surrogacy. Surrogacy was not the journey to parenthood I had imagined, but the end result would be the same: a family of our own. I would have traded all of my business success for a baby, so it felt like the right choice.

I was incredibly nervous about how people would react. The concept of surrogacy was a controversial topic in 2013. At the time, most of society didn't think it was "normal" to have kids through a surrogate because it was "not traditional." When my husband and I made the decision, there was still a lot of complexity and debate over the issue. It wasn't even legal in all fifty states. It still isn't as I'm writing this. In fact, it's only legal in four countries. I was worried that people would criticize and judge my journey into motherhood, but we cared about having kids more than anything in the world.

All of this added up to a tricky situation. If I explained my choice, I put myself at risk for potential judgment, criticism, and unwelcome commentary. I also would be forced to talk about my struggles with infertility, which was a deeply private and painful subject for me.

So I decided to tell no one.

I realized I didn't have to care what people thought about the choice I'd made for my family. I didn't need to prioritize other people's judgment over my desire to have kids. My husband and I were solid in our belief that we were making the best decision for the family we wanted to have, and we didn't need anyone else's input.

This turned out to be a wise move since nothing went as planned. Our surrogate became pregnant with twins, and a sudden infection caused both babies to be delivered at twenty-four weeks—three and a half months before their due date. Both of my children weighed only one pound. On top of their terrifying premature delivery, my son had a staph infection and brain bleed, and my daughter needed immediate open-heart surgery. Our doctors told us there was a good chance one or both of our babies wouldn't survive. Even if they did make it, they were so underdeveloped there was a chance they could be disabled for life.

There wasn't a single day in the fourteen weeks after they arrived that I didn't fear one or both of my twins was going to die. There were days I didn't want to get out of bed, let alone go to work, but I had no choice. I had two little babies who needed me as they fought for their lives. Outside of our immediate family, no one had any idea of the pain we were going through. No one saw my broken heart at work. Those days challenged my faith and optimism so much that it hurts to talk about it, even today.

Thankfully, my daughter's heart surgery was a success and my son's brain stopped bleeding before it permanently impacted him. Day by day, their health stabilized and they got stronger. Over the following months, our vision of having a family became a reality, and we were finally able to bring them home. They were fighters.

As my husband and I finally started breathing easy again and learning how to be parents, we were so grateful that we'd kept our news private. If we'd had to cope with judgment about the surrogacy *and* endless (well-meaning) questions about the health of our twins, we might've lost our minds.

We skipped telling people we were "expecting" and went straight to, "Guess what? We have twins!" And yes, that set us up to do a whole lot of explaining after the fact . . . but it was much easier to dismiss other people's judgment when I was holding my darling baby twins in my arms.

Regardless of whether your jump is a career jump or a personal jump, you need to be prepared to go against the grain—even if doing that makes people talk. Trust your own beliefs and opinions more than you value what other people think of you. Do your best to follow your north star and not get derailed by other people's whys, hows, and what-ifs.

You hold the key to your happiness; no one else does.

CUT OUT THE CRITICS

Every year I take time to reflect on the people I spend the most time with and determine if my circle is filled with the right people. I always want to have more optimists than pessimists, and sometimes that means weeding out a few lingering critics. I call this process a "life audit," and it is an essential step in setting yourself up for success. I sort people into two categories: (1) those who lift me up, and (2) those who bring me down. I write down the names of people who energize, challenge, inspire, and support me. Then I reflect on the people who are emotional vampires: the people in my life who complain, criticize, gossip, and drain my energy. If they aren't supporting me as I prepare for my next jump, I make an active choice to spend less time with them.

Whenever I do it, I always feel excited and energized to know that I am making a conscious decision to surround myself with optimists, people who will boost my confidence and self-esteem. You can't surround yourself with negative people and expect to lead a positive life. While this may sound like the kind of clinical, right-brain madness a tech entrepreneur would come up with, it's actually a very emotionally healthy process.

That said, it is never easy to distance yourself from negative people who are a part of your life. In fact, it is usually hard and painful, even when you know it's what is best for you. You can't always control other people's pessimistic attitudes, but you can control how much time you spend with them.

Some of my friends think it's a bit ruthless. I've learned there are limits to this concept and places where complexities and challenges arise. In these areas, it's important to consider setting boundaries as an alternative to auditing someone out completely. For instance, family relationships bring about a specific set of complexities. You might have parents, siblings, or cousins who criticize you. This can be especially painful because, more often than not, those are the very people whose approval you want. My suggestion in this case is to draw boundaries, limit the time you spend with them, and consider making certain topics that have a lot of emotional complexity "off-limits." If people challenge your choices, it is important to stay grounded and try to avoid being defensive. Here are some phrases that have helped me in the past:

- I'd prefer not to talk about that.

- I'm overwhelmed, and I need some time to think.

- I appreciate that you don't agree, and we just see things differently.

- I need to give this a try. Even if it fails, I don't want to look back with regret that I didn't try.

- If you don't agree, are you still willing to support my needs? Even if they are different from what you think I should do?

And, of course, people you love may hit tough times and become overwhelmingly negative . . . that's totally normal, and it's usually temporary! When these people are dealing with circumstances beyond their control—like illness, the death of someone close to them, or even the loss of a job—that's when you stick it out. They need you, and sometimes your positivity is the very thing that will help them through their negative experiences. Keep them close; don't push them away. Use your gut to decide whether someone is dealing with negativity in his or her own life and reflecting that outward for a short time . . . or whether he or she is just a negative person, through and through.

Now that you know the various ways this might play out, here are the basics of performing your own life audit:

1. List the five people you spend the most time with.

2. Look at each of their names, and really think about your relationship with them.

3. Who energizes you, inspires you, and lifts you up? Put a plus sign next to them.

4. Who complains, criticizes you, or adds negativity to your life? Put a minus sign next to them.

5. Commit to investing more time and energy into the positive relationships, and set boundaries to limit or eliminate the negative and toxic people.

There is no way to eradicate all negativity from your life, but you can limit it by controlling the number of negative *people* you allow into your life. You can make the tough but healthy choice to audit out anyone who drags you down with complaints, gossip, or criticism, and you can surround yourself with loving, supportive individuals who will cheer you on as you prepare for and take your jump.

Staying positive is a choice—not always an easy one in some relationships, but still a choice. That choice to stay positive is one you'll have to make again and again, in your social life, family life, and work life. It's not something you do once; it's a lifelong practice. But it's a practice that's well worth mastering.

IT'S NEVER TOO LATE TO JUMP

Innovation and inspiration can come at any age. It's time to rethink stereotypes and shut down the negative thinkers who say that monumental life changes can only be tackled by young people. What matters most is the desire to begin something of your own and the belief that it's possible. It's never too late (or too early) to start.

Sure, getting an early start on achievement has its advantages, but some of the most successful people in the world were late bloomers. Take Harland Sanders, the man who would later receive an honorary title and become the iconic Colonel Sanders, founder of KFC. He quit school in seventh grade, spent time in the army, and then held a variety of jobs before opening Sanders' Cafe across the street from a service station in Corbin, Kentucky. He was forty years old when this restaurant opened its doors to the hungry public. There, he perfected his recipe for "finger lickin' good chicken" by using a secret blend of eleven herbs and spices and a pressure cooker to seal in the flavors.[5] (Is your mouth watering yet?)

In 1952, Sanders was sixty-two years old, and he began actively franchising his chicken business. The first Kentucky Fried Chicken restaurant opened in Salt Lake City, after which Sanders sold Sanders' Cafe and started traveling across the country to broker more franchising deals. He would personally cook batches of his chicken at each restaurant, and the owners who signed on to use his recipe paid him a nickel for every chicken they sold. By 1964—when Sanders was seventy-four and had more than six hundred franchised outlets—he sold his interest in the company for $2 million and retired.[6] (That's nearly $17 million in today's dollars!)

Colonel Sanders's story is proof that entrepreneurship knows no age. He worked hard his whole life, but he only hit it big when he was in his sixties and began thinking like a businessman.

According to findings from the National Bureau of Economic Research, the average entrepreneur is forty years old, and the average age of leaders of high-growth startups is forty-five years old. That's right—not only can you start a business at any age, but age is actually a *predictor* of entrepreneurial success.

And when it comes to taking bold risks and embracing life-changing jumps, you're never too old or too young. The world is changing faster than ever, and no matter your age, you can change right along with it.

We're at the crest of a massive wave of people making transformational life changes and taking the leap to become their own bosses. The *Wall Street Journal* reported that

Americans are starting new businesses at the fastest rate in over a decade and choosing to become solopreneurs in increasing numbers. Statista estimates that by 2027, 86.5 million people will be freelancing in the United States, which is an amazing 50.9 percent of the total US workforce.

With millions already working for themselves and tens of millions more aiming to do so within the next five years, it's clear that the world is undergoing a permanent shift in the way we work. We no longer inhabit a world where our opportunities are defined by where we live. Achieving our goals is made easier by our interconnectedness. It's a digital world, and there is no going back.

More and more people are looking for flexibility, freedom, and control over their time. We all want work that fuels our passion and gives life meaning. And it doesn't matter who you are, where you come from, or how old you are; you can bring those things into your life. Taking a jump is for anyone who wants to join the movement and has the guts to try.

If you're over forty and worried that you've missed your window for jumping, I'm here to tell you that window is still wide open. Don't let anyone tell you there's an expiration date on transformative change. For instance, many people have shifted gears or started businesses in their later years—and many have seen incredible success. In addition to Colonel Sanders, here are a few more you may have heard of:

Chip Wilson: You may not recognize the name Chip Wilson, but you're likely familiar with Lululemon. He founded the multibillion-dollar athleisure company at age forty-two.

Mary Stuart Masterson: This successful actress made a pivot toward entrepreneurship by founding Stockade Works, her production studio and trade school for actors and film professionals, at age fifty.[7]

Sam Walton: The company Sam Walton founded at age forty-four eventually became the largest private employer in the world and made him one of the richest men in the United States. That company? Walmart.

My father: At the young age of seventy-two, my dad is currently starting a new business building carbon-neutral housing. He's a lifelong entrepreneur who has started all sorts of ventures, but even after all these years, he is still energized by starting something new.

Of course, it's never too early to become an entrepreneur either. My nine-year-old niece currently has a business selling dog treats in her neighborhood, and that's not even the first business she's ever started. She says her current venture combines two of her greatest passions—talking to people and helping animals.

So, whether you're nine, seventy-two, or anywhere in between, be confident that you absolutely *can* make this jump happen, no matter what your age, the status quo, or what anyone else says.

Chapter 9 Jump Prep

- If you're a people-pleaser, identify where your people-pleasing tendencies are getting in your way of making your jump. Where do you go out of your way to make others feel comfortable, even if it means sacrificing your own valuable time or resources? When do you say yes when you want desperately to say no? Where are you wasting time and energy, consumed by worry because you've upset someone in your life? What is one action you can take to start living life for *yourself* instead of for others?

- Try one of the activities to accentuate the positive. Keeping a gratitude journal, savoring the moment, and mindfulness exercises will all help you resist the downward drag of criticism and negativity.

- Perform your life audit! If you don't do it now, set a date in your calendar to do it in the next week.

Chapter 9 Jump Hacks

- Although most of the negativity we discussed in this chapter comes from people you know, there's plenty more to be had online in the form of news, comments, and internet clickbait. So turn off your notifications for five hours every day. Cut out the noise, and limit your media consumption to see how it impacts your emotional well-being.

- When you receive constructive feedback—about your jump or anything else—do your best to view it as your opportunity to improve. Thank the people offering feed-back for their opinions, decide if the feedback is relevant and important to take on board, and then move forward. Feedback can be a gift, but only if you're prepared to treat it as one.

- Stockpile those positive moments! Even if a gratitude journal doesn't appeal to you, consider creating a diary or electronic document filled with praise, good experiences, and new discoveries. Turn to it whenever you're feeling scared or doubtful.

- Reach out to five people in your life and ask them what your superpowers are. Remind yourself of the magic you already have!

CHAPTER

10

READY. SET. JUMP!

This is it.

It's time to commit to getting started. It's time to begin. You need to go for it. Reject stagnation, and *jump*. The first step you take will be intimidating, but I promise it makes the second easier.

Because a path leads to a path.

Once you overcome your fears and push aside your hesitation, endless paths will unfold at your feet. You'll see how movement and action lead to possibilities in ways that stillness and rumination never can.

If you're still scared, that's totally understandable. Change is scary, and a life-altering jump is nothing to take lightly. But I don't want your fear to stop you, and I don't want you to wait until you're no longer afraid. Instead, use that fear as fuel to transform your life! Focus on feeling your fear and forging ahead anyway.

You've got all the knowledge, the principles, and a kick-ass one-year success plan. Now it's time to apply your energy. Get started and build momentum. Make the jump.

If you've ever studied physics, you likely know the law of inertia. Simply put, it states that a body in motion tends to stay in motion while a body at rest tends to stay at rest, unless acted upon by another force. You've got to be that force. And guess what: just like with Newton's law, once you're moving, you'll find it's easier to keep moving.

What you envision for yourself now will likely change and evolve as you move forward. When it does, you can always pivot, or you can jump again if you need to. The great news is that the fear you feel now will diminish each time you jump and experience change, success, and transformation. By committing to take *this* jump, you are setting yourself up for a lifetime of exploration and learning. When you take *this* jump, you will create the space for endless possibilities.

And remember, innovation and inspiration can come at any age. What matters most is the desire to begin something of your own and the belief that it's possible. It's never too late (or too early) to start.

You truly do have the power to change any aspect of your life, no matter what might be holding you back. Feel the fear and do it anyway.

Ready?

Set?

JUMP!

ACKNOWLEDGMENTS

I am deeply grateful to all the people who helped me achieve my vision for this book. From brainstorming its concept to editing its many drafts and turning it into a book I'm deeply proud of.

Thank you to . . .

My husband, John, for your unconditional love, support, and being the best partner who always says yes to any adventure. My story wouldn't be the same without you.

My four inspiring children, Elle, John, Bill, and Jack, who are the source of pure joy, laughter, and love in my life. I'm in awe watching you grow and can't wait to support the dreams you will chase and the mountains you will climb.

My parents, for being incredible role models, sounding boards, and the most important teachers of my life.

My twin sister, Tracy, for being an incredible editor and collaborator, and for always remembering the stories that helped us grow.

My brother Mark, for being a constant anchor of support and encouragement.

Sherry, thank you for your unwavering support, invaluable feedback, and for always paying attention to every detail.

Amanda, I'd be lost without your talent for knowing everything that's happening in the world and the perfect way to tie it into a great story. I'm so grateful for your friendship and wisdom.

Liv, I don't know what I would do without you. Writing this book has been a journey, and you've been there from the beginning. I am so grateful for your writing talents and your bringing humor and sanity to the chaos of book writing.

My wonderful family and friends, for your continued support and encouragement through all the jumps I've taken in my life and career. I wouldn't have landed without you.

All of my mentors, for your priceless guidance and wisdom throughout my life.

Chris, for giving me a masterclass in branding, mentorship, and friendship at every turn.

My incredible team at HarperCollins, for believing in my idea and providing invaluable guidance and advice.

The remarkable leaders whom I had the opportunity to work with and for—and all the entrepreneurs I have been fortunate to invest in—for allowing me to learn from you.

And finally, for my readers, I wrote this with the hope of helping you jump and achieve the success and happiness you've always dreamed of.

NOTES

Chapter 1: Take the Leap

1. "Briogeo's Nancy Twine on Building a Hair Care Brand," *Life with Marianna* podcast, March 9, 2021. Accessed at https://podcasts.apple.com /us/podcast/briogeos-nancy-twine-on-building-a-hair-care-brand /id1538242507?i=1000512206509.
2. Gianna Capadone, "Briogeo's Nancy Twine: 'The Challenge of Working with Retailers Is We Don't Get Customer Data," *The Glossy Beauty Podcast*, April 18, 2019. Accessed at https://www.glossy.co/podcasts /briogeos-nancy-twine-the-challenge-of-working-with-retailers-is-we -dont-get-customer-data/.
3. Nathan McAlone, "This Man Invented the Digital Camera in 1975—and His Bosses at Kodak Never Let It See the Light of Day," *Business Insider*, August 17, 2015. Accessed at https://www.businessinsider.com/this-man -invented-the-digital-camera-in-1975-and-his-bosses-at-kodak-never-let -it-see-the-light-of-day-2015-8.
4. Susie Steiner, "The 5 Things People Regret Most on Their Deathbed," *Business Insider*, December 5, 2013. Accessed at https://www.businessinsider .com/5-things-people-regret-on-their-deathbed-2013-12.
5. Bryan Goodwin, "Research Matters: The Magic of Writing Stuff Down," *Educational Leadership*, April 2018. Accessed at http://www.ascd.org /publications/educational-leadership/apr18/vol75/num07/The-Magic -of-Writing-Stuff-Down.aspx.
6. "Eleanor Roosevelt Biography," FDR Library. Accessed at https://www .fdrlibrary.org/eleanor-roosevelt.

Chapter 2: Master Your Mindset

1. Jenny Lawson, "Pretend You're Good at It: Thoughts on Recording LET'S PRETEND THIS NEVER HAPPENED: A Mostly True Memoir," *Book Reporter*, June 4, 2012. Accessed at https://www.bookreporter.com /blog/2012/06/04/pretend-youre-good-at-it-thoughts-on-recording-lets -pretend-this-never-happened-a-mo.

2. Burt Helm, "How I Did It: James Dyson," *Inc.*, February 28, 2012. Accessed at https://www.inc.com/magazine/201203/burt-helm/how-i-did-it-james -dyson.html.

3. Madison Malone-Kircher, "James Dyson on 5,126 Vacuums That Didn't Work—and the One That Finally Did," *New York*, November 22, 2016. Accessed at https://nymag.com/vindicated/2016/11/james-dyson-on-5 -126-vacuums-that-didnt-work-and-1-that-did.html.

4. Madison Malone-Kircher, "James Dyson on 5,126 Vacuums That Didn't Work—and the One That Finally Did."

5. "Sir James Dyson: From Barrows to Billions," BBC News, April 22, 2021. Accessed at https://www.bbc.com/news/business-46149743.

6. Sir James Dyson, "No Innovator's Dilemma Here: In Praise of Failure," *Wired*, April 8, 2011. Accessed at https://www.wired.com/2011/04 /in-praise-of-failure/.

7. "#234 James Dyson," Billionaires 2021, *Forbes*, May 11, 2021. Accessed at https://www.forbes.com/profile/james-dyson/?sh=1856fa4b2b38.

8. Dr. Margie Warrell, "How Are Your Excuses Costing You?" blog entry, September 11, 2009. Accessed at https://margiewarrell.com /are-you-stuck-in-excuses/.

9. Christopher Clarey, "Olympians Use Imagery as Mental Training," *New York Times*, February 22, 2014. Accessed at https://www.nytimes .com/2014/02/23/sports/olympics/olympians-use-imagery-as-mental -training.html.

10. Rick Maese, "For Olympians, Seeing (In Their Minds) Is Believing (It Can Happen)," *Washington Post*, July 28, 2016. Accessed at https://www .washingtonpost.com/sports/olympics/for-olympians-seeing-in-their -minds-is-believing-it-can-happen/2016/07/28/6966709c-532e-11e6-bbf5 -957ad17b4385_story.html.

11. Traci Sitzmann and Gillian Yeo, "A Meta-Analytic Investigation of the Within-Person Self-Efficacy Domain: Is Self-Efficacy a Product of Past Performance or a Driver of Future Performance?" *Personal Psychology* 66(3), September 2013. Accessed at https://www.researchgate .net/publication/264479041_A_Meta-Analytic_Investigation_of_the _Within-Person_Self-Efficacy_Domain_Is_Self-Efficacy_a_Product_of _Past_Performance_or_a_Driver_of_Future_Performance.

12. Dixie Gillaspie, "You'll Never Accomplish Goals You Don't Really Care About," *Entrepreneur*, January 20, 2017. Accessed at https://www .entrepreneur.com/article/254371#:~:text=In%20fact%2C%20in%20a%20 report,don't%20write%20them%20down.

Chapter 3: Turn Your Fears into Fuel

1. Michael Guta, "33% of Americans Say Fear of Failure Holds Them Back from Starting a Business," Small Business Trends, November 16, 2018. Accessed at https://smallbiztrends.com/2018/11/fear-of-failure-in -business.html.

2. Gillian Zoe Segal, "This Self-Made Billionaire Failed the LSAT Twice, Then Sold Fax Machines for 7 Years Before Hitting Big—Here's How She Got There," CNBC *Make It*, April 3, 2019. Accessed at https://www.cnbc .com/2019/04/03/self-made-billionaire-spanx-founder-sara-blakely-sold -fax-machines-before-making-it-big.html.
3. Kathy Caprino, "10 Lessons I Learned from Sara Blakely That You Won't Hear in Business School," *Forbes*, May 23, 2012. Accessed at https://www .forbes.com/sites/kathycaprino/2012/05/23/10-lessons-i-learned-from -sara-blakely-that-you-wont-hear-in-business-school/?sh=4235ee1c1438.
4. "How a Pitch in a Neiman Marcus Ladies Room Changed Sara Blakely's Life," NPR transcript, September 12, 2016. Accessed at https://www.npr .org/transcripts/493312213.
5. Accessed at https://www.forbes.com/sites/clareoconnor/2012/03/07 /undercover-billionaire-sara-blakely-joins-the-rich-list-thanks-to-spanx /?sh=37961110d736.
6. Clare O'Connor, "Undercover Billionaire: Sara Blakely Joins the Rich List Thanks to Spanx," *Forbes*, May 7, 2012. Accessed at https://www.forbes .com/profile/sara-blakely/?sh=6704762476bb.
7. "Aren't Sure? Brain Is Primed for Learning," *Yale News*, July 19, 2018. Accessed at https://news.yale.edu/2018/07/19/arent-sure -brain-primed-learning.
8. Alix Spiegel and Micaela Rodriguez, "Eager to Burst His Own Bubble, a Techie Made Apps to Randomize His Life," NPR *Morning Edition*, June 8, 2017. Accessed at https://www.npr.org/sections /alltechconsidered/2017/06/08/531796329/eager-to-burst-his-own-bubble -a-techie-made-apps-to-randomize-his-life.
9. Max Hawkins, "Randomized Living," n.d. Accessed at https://maxhawkins .me/work/randomized_living.
10. Nancy C. Andreason, "Secrets of the Creative Brain," *Atlantic*, July/ August 2014. Accessed at https://www.theatlantic.com/magazine/archive /2014/07/secrets-of-the-creative-brain/372299/.
11. Jeff Shore, "Why Should You Embrace Discomfort? Opportunity, Of Course," *Entrepreneur*, April 30, 2014. Accessed at https://www.entrepreneur.com /article/233514.
12. Stephen Rodrick, "Chris Rock in a Hard Place: On Infidelity, His New Tour and Starting Over," *Rolling Stone*, May 3, 2017. Accessed at https://www .rollingstone.com/tv/tv-features/chris-rock-in-a-hard-place-on-infidelity -his-new-tour-and-starting-over-114653/.
13. "Worst I Bombed Ever: Chris Rock," *The Tonight Show Starring Jimmy Fallon*, YouTube, posted May 3, 2017. Accessed at https://www.youtube .com/watch?v=Cxli8mBfn6c.
14. Ja Jiang, "What I Learned from 100 Days of Rejection," TED Talk, May 2015. Accessed at https://www.ted.com/talks/jia_jiang_what _i_learned_from_100_days_of_rejection?language=en.
15. Ja Jiang, "What I Learned from 100 Days of Rejection."

16. Bryan E. Robinson, "The 90-Second Rule That Builds Self-Control," *Psychology Today*, April 26, 2020. Accessed at https://www.psychologytoday.com/us/blog/the-right-mindset/202004/the-90-second-rule-builds-self-control.

Chapter 4: The Power of Decision-Making

1. Tom Huddleston Jr., "Netflix Didn't Kill Blockbuster—How Netflix Almost Lost the Movie Rental Wars," CNBC *Make It*, September 22, 2020. Accessed at https://www.cnbc.com/2020/09/22/how-netflix-almost-lost-the-movie-rental-wars-to-blockbuster.html.
2. Miguel Helft, "Netflix to Deliver Movies to the PC," *New York Times*, January 16, 2007. Accessed at https://www.nytimes.com/2007/01/16/technology/16netflix.html.
3. "Netflix's Net Income from 2000 to 2020," Statista, March 18, 2021. Accessed at https://www.statista.com/statistics/272561/netflix-net-income/.
4. Clay Skipper, "How to Be Better at Being Wrong," *GQ*, February 15, 2018. Accessed at https://www.gq.com/story/annie-duke-thinking-in-bets-how-to-be-wrong-interview.
5. Clay Skipper, "How to Be Better at Being Wrong."
6. Shabnam Mousavi and Gerd Gigerenzer, "Risk, Uncertainty, and Heuristics," *Journal of Business Research* 67(8), August 2014, 1671–78. Accessed at https://www.sciencedirect.com/science/article/abs/pii/S0148296314000885.
7. Zohair Swaine, "Colin Powell's 40/70 Approach to Leadership and Executive Decisions," *Financial Advisor*, October 2, 2017. Accessed at https://www.fa-mag.com/news/colin-powell-s-40-70-approach-to-leadership-and-executive-decisions-34956.html.
8. "Tina Fey's Aha! Moment," *O, The Oprah Magazine*, June 2003. Accessed at https://www.oprah.com/spirit/tina-feys-aha-moment.

Chapter 5: Define Success on Your Own Terms

1. Miranda Bryant, "Reddit Co-founder on Paternity Leave and Male Success: 'These Things Are Not Mutually Exclusive,'" *Guardian*, January 29, 2020. Accessed at https://www.theguardian.com/us-news/2020/jan/29/alexis-ohanian-paternity-leave-male-success-these-things-are-not-mutually-exclusive.
2. Accessed at https://www.chicagotribune.com/business/ct-biz-zalando-ceo-quits-career-wife-20201207-fkyme3fcnjbztaiw572i2miyme-story.htm.
3. Shana Leibowitz and Allana Akhtar, "14 Rich and Powerful People Share Their Surprising Definitions of Success," *Business Insider*, May 29, 2019. Accessed at https://www.businessinsider.com/how-successful-people-define-success-2017-3#inventor-thomas-edison-recognized-that-success-is-a-grind-10.

Chapter 6: Create Your One-Year Success Plan

1. "Anybody Can Run: The Story of Couch to 5k," BBC News, September 12, 2018. Accessed at https://www.bbc.com/news/av/stories-45485776.
2. Josh Clark, "How Josh Clark Invented 'Couch to 5k' and Helped Millions Start Running," Big Medium, September 25, 2018. Accessed at https://bigmedium.com/ideas/bbc-how-josh-clark-invented-couch-to-5k.html.
3. Josh Clark, "How Josh Clark Invented 'Couch to 5k' and Helped Millions Start Running."
4. Scott Allison, "Mastering the Rockefeller Habits—How to Scale a Hyper-Growth Business," *Forbes*, August 31, 2012. Accessed at https://www.forbes.com/sites/scottallison/2012/08/31/mastering-the-rockefeller-habits-how-to-scale-a-hyper-growth-business/?sh=1a784139af5e.

Chapter 7: The Art of Relationship Building

1. "Workplace Loyalties Change, but the Value of Mentoring Doesn't," Knowledge@Wharton, May 16, 2007. Accessed at https://knowledge.wharton.upenn.edu/article/workplace-loyalties-change-but-the-value-of-mentoring-doesnt/.
2. "Why Mentoring: What the Stats Say," McCarthy Mentoring, May 2017. Accessed at https://mccarthymentoring.com/why-mentoring-what-the-stats-say/.
3. Anjuli Sastry and Andee Tagle, "The Right Mentor Can Change Your Career. Here's How to Find One," NPR, September 3, 2020. Accessed at https://www.npr.org/2019/10/25/773158390/how-to-find-a-mentor-and-make-it-work.
4. Imran Tariq, "4 Details for Successful Networking That Most People Overlook," *Entrepreneur*, January 13, 2020. Accessed at https://www.entrepreneur.com/article/343747.

Chapter 8: Tap into Your Inner Strength

1. Rebecca Johnson, "Senator Tammy Duckworth on the Attack That Took Her Legs—And Having a Baby at 50," *Vogue*, September 12, 2018. Accessed at https://www.vogue.com/article/tammy-duckworth-interview-vogue-october-2018-issue.
2. Tammy Duckworth, official Senate site. Accessed at https://www.duckworth.senate.gov/about-tammy/biography.
3. "Tammy Duckworth," Biography, April 10, 2018 (updated August 3, 2020). Accessed at https://www.biography.com/political-figure/tammy-duckworth.
4. Erin Jensen, "5 Takeaways on Vulnerability from Brené Brown's 'The Call to Courage,'" *USA Today*, April 19, 2019. Accessed at https://www.usatoday.com/story/life/tv/2019/04/19/brene-brown-call-courage-netflix-vulnerability/3497969002/.

5. Rebecca J. Rosen, "Sheryl Sandberg's Advice for Grieving," *Atlantic*, April 28, 2017. Accessed at https://www.theatlantic.com/business /archive/2017/04/sandberg-optionb/524640/.

6. Tasra Sophia Mohr, "Why Women Don't Apply for Jobs Unless They're 100% Qualified," *Harvard Business Review*, August 25, 2014. Accessed at https://hbr.org/2014/08/why-women-dont-apply -for-jobs-unless-theyre-100-qualified.

7. Katty Kay and Claire Shipman, "The Confidence Gap," *Atlantic*, May, 2014. Accessed at https://www.theatlantic.com/magazine/archive/2014/05 /the-confidence-gap/359815/.

8. Rohit Bargava, "Timing—The Most Creative Lunch in History," excerpt from *Likeonomics* posted at author's website, May 26, 2012. Accessed at https://www.rohitbhargava.com/2012/05/timing-the-most-creative -lunch-in-history.html.

Chapter 9: Stop Caring What Other People Think

1. Amrisha Vaish, Tobias Grossmann, and Amanda Woodward, "Not All Emotions Are Created Equal: The Negativity Bias in Social-Emotional Development," *Psychological Bulletin* 134(3), May 2008, 383–403. Accessed at https://www.ncbi.nlm.nih.gov/pmc/articles/PMC3652533/.

2. Hara Estroff Marano, "Our Brain's Negative Bias," *Psychology Today*, June 20, 2003 (updated June 9, 2016). Accessed at https://www .psychologytoday.com/us/articles/200306/our-brains-negative-bias.

3. "What Is Gratitude?" *Greater Good Magazine*, n.d. Accessed at https://greatergood.berkeley.edu/topic/gratitude/definition#why -practice-gratitude.

4. Russ Harris, *The Confidence Gap: A Guide to Overcoming Fear and Self-Doubt* (Durban, South Africa: Trumpeter, 2011), 178.

5. "Harland Sanders," Britannica, n.d. Accessed at https://www.britannica .com/biography/Harland-Sanders.

6. "Colonel Harland Sanders," Biography, April 27, 2017 (updated April 24, 2020). Accessed at https://www.biography.com/business-figure /colonel-harland-sanders.

7. Leander Schaerlaeckens, "Mary Stuart Masterson: Entrepreneur and Actress," *Upstater* magazine, Summer 2016. Accessed at https://upstater .com/mary-stuart-mastrson-entrepreneur-actress/.

INDEX